ESSENTIAL
SURVIVAL
SKILLS

KEY TIPS AND TECHNIQUES
FOR THE GREAT OUTDOORS

Includes content previously published in
The Survival Handbook: Essential Skills for Outdoor Adventure

DK

LONDON, NEW YORK, MUNICH,
MELBOURNE, and DELHI

Senior Editor Bob Bridle
Senior Art Editor Sharon Spencer
Production Editor Tony Phipps
Production Controller Louise Minihane
Jacket Designer Mark Cavanagh
Managing Editor Stephanie Farrow
Managing Art Editor Lee Griffiths
US Editor Margaret Parrish

DK INDIA

Managing Art Editor Ashita Murgai
Editorial Lead Saloni Talwar
Senior Art Editor Rajnish Kashyap
Project Designer Akanksha Gupta
Project Editor Samira Sood
Designers Avani Parikh, Neetika Vilash
Editors Shatarupa Chaudhuri, Pallavi Singh
DTP Manager Balwant Singh
Senior DTP Designer Harish Aggarwal
DTP Designers Shanker Prasad, Vishal Bhatia, Bimlesh Tiwari
Managing Director Aparna Sharma

First American Edition, 2011

Published in the United States by
DK Publishing
375 Hudson Street
New York, New York 10014
12 13 14 15 10 9 8 7 6 5 4 3 2

004—SD400—Mar/2011

Includes content previously published in
*The Survival Handbook: Essential Skills
for Outdoor Adventure*

A catalog record for this book
is available from the Library of Congress

Important Notice
Some of the techniques described in this book should
be used only in dire emergencies, when the survival of
individuals depends upon them. The publisher cannot
be held responsible for any injuries, damage, loss, or
prosecutions resulting from the use or misuses of
the information in this book. Do not practice these
techniques on private land without the owner's
permission, and obey all laws relating to the protection
of land, property, plants, and animals.

ISBN 978-0-7566-5998-1

DK books are available at special discounts when
purchased in bulk for sales promotions, premiums,
fund-raising, or educational use. For details, contact:
DK Publishing Special Markets, 375 Hudson Street,
New York, New York 10014 or SpecialSales@dk.com.

Printed and bound by
L. Rex Printing Company Limited, China

Discover more at www.dk.com

Contents

Introduction

Having taught survival skills for many years, I have learned that four elements must be in place for a survival situation to have the chance of a positive outcome: knowledge, ability, the will to survive, and luck. While knowledge and ability can be learned, the will to survive is hard-wired into our survival mechanism, and we may not know we possess it until we're put to the test. For example, people who were fully trained and well-equipped have given up hope in survivable conditions, while others, who were less well-prepared and ill-equipped, have survived against all odds because they refused to give up.

> ❝ ALWAYS APPLY THE PRINCIPLE OF THE **LEAST AMOUNT OF ENERGY EXPENDED** FOR THE **MAXIMUM AMOUNT OF GAIN**. ❞

Anyone venturing into the wilderness—whether for an overnight camping trip or a lengthy expedition—should understand the basic principles of survival. Knowing how to survive in a particular situation will allow you to carry out the correct beforehand preparation, choose the right equipment (and learn how to use it), and practice the necessary skills. While you may be able to start a fire using a lighter, for example, what would you do if it stopped working? Equally, anyone can spend a comfortable night inside a one-man bivi shelter, but what would you do if you lost your pack? The knowledge gained through learning the skills of survival will enable you to assess your situation, prioritize your needs, and improvise any items of gear that you don't have with you.

Survival knowledge and skills must be learned—and practiced—under realistic conditions. Starting a fire with dry materials on a sunny day, for example, will teach you very little. The real survival skill is in understanding why a fire won't start and working out a solution. The more you practice, the more you learn (I am yet to teach a course where I didn't learn something new from one of my students). Finding solutions and overcoming problems continually adds to your knowledge and, in most cases, will help you deal with problems should they occur again.

As you read this book and plan to put the skills and techniques covered here into practice, you will typically be equipping yourself for just one particular type of environment—but it's important that you fully understand that one environment. Make sure you research not only what the environment has to offer you as a traveler—so that you can better appreciate it—but also what it offers you as a survivor: there is, sometimes, a very thin line between being in awe of the beauty of an environment and being at its mercy. The more you understand both the appeal and dangers of an environment, the better informed you will be to select the right equipment and understand how best to utilize it should the need arise.

Remember, no matter how good your survival equipment, or how extensive your knowledge and skills, never underestimate the power of nature. If things aren't going as planned, never hesitate to stop and reassess your situation and priorities, and never be afraid to turn back and try again later—the challenge will always be there tomorrow. Finally, you must always remember that the most effective method of dealing with a survival situation is to avoid getting into it in the first place.

COLIN TOWELL

THERE IS A THIN LINE BETWEEN BEING IN AWE OF AN ENVIRONMENT AND BEING AT ITS MERCY.

Before You Go

Before You Go

Most survival situations arise in one of two ways: either you are thrust into a situation not of your making and beyond your control, or a situation develops because of a sequence of events that could have been avoided had you recognized the danger signs and acted on them at the earliest opportunity. Unfortunately, most survival situations occur as a result of ignorance, arrogance, or because the forces of nature have been underestimated.

Whether you're preparing for an overnight camping trip or a year-long trip around Africa, the more prepared you are to meet the challenges posed by a particular environment, the more likely you are to be able to cope—both physically and mentally—if you should then find yourself confronted with a survival situation.

It is equally important to choose the correct equipment and clothing. When selecting gear, think about what you would need to survive if the worst happened. This is your "first-line" equipment, which you should carry with you at all times. It should enable you to address the basic principles of survival relevant to the environment you are in, and consists of the clothing you would wear and your basic survival equipment—your survival tin and belt-order (see pp.34–35).

Before you head off, double-check that your gear works and that you know how to use it properly. The more you understand how and why a piece of equipment works, the better able you will be to improvise if it gets damaged or lost.

> ❝ NEVER ASSUME THAT THE AMOUNT OF **PRIOR PREPARATION** REQUIRED IS DIRECTLY RELATED TO THE LENGTH OF A TRIP OR ITS **PERCEIVED DANGER**. ❞

Using a walking stick

A walking stick is one of the simplest yet most important survival aids you will ever need. It's the first piece of equipment to improvise if you find yourself in a survival situation.

The "survivor's third leg"—as a walking stick is also known—increases your ability to support yourself by allowing you to have two points of contact with the ground at any one time. This will reduce the chance of you slipping—a crucial factor given that your ability to walk may be your main means of rescue; reduce your mobility and you seriously reduce your ability to survive.

A versatile tool, your walking stick can be employed in many different survival situations. Among its many uses, it can be used to:

- Support you as you walk
- Protect your face when you're walking through thickets or gorse
- Check for adequate support when you're crossing marshy ground
- Test the ground ahead for obstructions
- Check the depth of water when crossing streams and rivers
- Protect you against wild animals
- Form a ridgepole for your shelter
- Help you with your pace counting
- Spear fish or catch game
- Dig up roots or plants

Mental preparation

On any trip or expedition, your situation can change for the worse. Quickly moving into the unknown can cause tremendous psychological and emotional stress, known as "psychogenic shock." Understanding this will help you deal with it better and reduce its impact.

Your response to disaster situations

Your psychological response to a survival situation is crucial. If you break down psychologically, your chances of overcoming a situation will be compromised.

PSYCHOLOGICAL PROGRESSION	
It's useful to examine how people are likely to react in a survival situation. You can use this knowledge to prepare mentally for such eventualities. Normal psychological reactions to disaster tend to occur in a set pattern (see below). Contrary to popular belief, people don't normally panic, although it can be contagious if someone does.	
Pre-impact period	This is divided into two stages: • Threat: danger exists but, although obvious to those who recognize it, those who will not accept it respond with denial and under-activity. • Warning: threat of danger is now apparent to all; response is now likely to be over-activity.
Impact period	This is the life-threatening stage. Statistically, individuals behave in one of three ways: • 10–20 percent of people are calm and retain full awareness. • Up to 75 percent of people are stunned, bewildered, and unable to react rationally. • 10–25 percent exhibit extreme behavior, such as screaming.
Recoil period	This follows on directly from the impact period; for example, victims may have escaped a sinking ship and are in liferafts. It can be between three hours and three days. Most often, it is characterized by a gradual return to normal reasoning abilities, awareness, and emotional expression.
Post-trauma period	If the recoil period is not fully successful, individuals may develop psychiatric disorders. The full impact of the incident becomes apparent and a range of emotions—guilt, depression, anxiety, and aimlessness—may develop. These are often called Post-Traumatic Stress Disorders (PTSD).

Individual reactions to disaster

People react to survival situations in different ways, although you can expect to find some common emotional reactions in victims. You may experience one or more of them during or after any survival experience.

PANIC
Panic arises from the fear of what might happen. It tends to occur when people are trapped, or if there is a time limit to their escape.

DEPRESSION
Depressed people will sit among chaos and debris, vacantly gazing and not replying to questions. They're unaware of their situation and unable to help themselves, so risk further injury.

HYPERACTIVITY
Hyperactive victims are easily distracted, and are full of chatter, ideas, and often unhelpful suggestions.

ANGER
Aggression, anger, and hostility are common reactions. They are often irrational and may even be directed at the rescuers or medical staff.

GUILT
Some sufferers feel guilty for surviving, and for not having done enough for others—and some irrationally blame themselves for bringing about the incident.

SUICIDE
Disaster victims have been known to commit suicide immediately after being rescued. Victims should be monitored.

❝ MOST PEOPLE WHO DIE WITH PSYCHOLOGICAL TRAUMA DIE WITHIN THE FIRST THREE DAYS. ❞

Aggravating factors

Reactions to disaster can result from a direct psychological blow, such as extreme shock, but they can also be brought on, or aggravated, by other factors. As with all psychological problems, knowing what these factors are, and attempting to avoid them, will maximize your chances of preventing or overcoming the problem.

COMMON AGGRAVATING FACTORS	
Hunger	Initially, hunger is not a problem, but a long-term lack of food will cause psychological changes to occur. Symptoms include: • Apathy • Irritability • Depression • Lack of concentration
Thirst	Thirst is a serious problem, especially for survivors at sea or in the desert. Agitation is commonplace; other symptoms include: • Irrational behavior (see box, right) • Delusions • Visual hallucinations
Fatigue	Physical exhaustion may be present from the outset, or may result from sleep deprivation and the physical hardship endured over time. Most survivors agree that fatigue overwhelms them, but when they want to sleep they can't—they are unable to relax. Fatigue causes a deterioration in mental and physical performance.
Sea-sickness	Seasickness often brings about an overwhelming desire to curl up and die, which, in survival situations, can easily become a reality. Fight seasickness with these methods: • Keep a fixed point such as the horizon in sight. • Take small sips of water (not salt water) if you have sufficient supplies, but ration them if you're in a life or death situation.
Hypothermia	This produces physical and psychological effects—the psychological consequences occur early in the condition, and cause: • Loss of concentration • Loss of memory • Motor impairment • Faulty decision-making • Irrational behavior

❝ THIRST IS A SERIOUS PROBLEM, AND ITS EFFECTS ARE MORE ACUTE THAN **THOSE OF HUNGER**. ❞

Coping strategies

There are many things you can do to prepare yourself psychologically for a survival situation. As with all survival skills, prior knowledge is power, and will help you to deal with a survival situation far more successfully. Developing coping strategies is an important technique for survival.

KEY COPING STRATEGIES	
Training	People who are prepared, who know their environment and how to use their equipment, and who understand what to expect in a survival situation, will be far more effective if they find themselves in one.
Motivation	Also called "the will to survive," this means refusing to accept death. It involves overcoming extreme emotional and physical discomfort. It is linked to the ability to set goals and work toward those goals.
Attachment	One of the strongest motivating forces for survival is the desire to be reunited with principal figures of attachment in your life. These may include: • Husbands • Wives • Partners • Children • Grandchildren • Close friends
Hope	In a survival situation, it's vital to cling on to hope, despite information or perceptions to the contrary. Thinking positively will help ward off psychological trauma.
Acceptance	Accepting a situation doesn't equate to giving in to it. Those who have this ability, and know when to be active and when passive, often have a better chance of survival.
Helping others	First, monitor your own condition and check that you're really up to the task. See who is genuinely disturbed—monitor them closely. Simple words of comfort and interest will make the majority who are numbed more responsive. Avoid giving sedatives.

IRRATIONAL BEHAVIOR

This can take many forms. Examples include the earthquake victims found collecting flowers instead of helping the injured; and the band of the Titanic, which played while the ship sank rather than trying to save themselves.

Planning your journey

Whether your trip involves a day out with your backpack, or an expedition over weeks, you need to plan it carefully. It's useful to have a basic planning outline for your most regular trips, to which you can add supplementary information as your trips become more involved.

Minimizing the "if only"

You can't plan for every eventuality on your trip, but you can look at the type of trip you intend to take, and ensure that if a situation arises, you're not left wishing you'd done something differently. While planning your trip, look at the potential problems and risks, plan to avoid them, and equip yourself with the knowledge and/or tools to deal with them.

WARNING

The social customs of every country are different. In some cases, ignoring them may lead to a penalty, punishment, or even imprisonment. Always research a country's customs when planning your trip.

The six P's

Remember the six P's: Prior Planning and Preparation Prevents Poor Performance. In many ways, a good understanding of how to deal with a situation, and the ability to interpret basic principles of survival, can prevent a minor problem from escalating into a disaster. Knowledge, and your ability to improvise, could determine your fate.

ORGANIZATIONAL PRIORITIES

When planning a trip, start with the most important things—the "show-stoppers." These are generally the things that would stop the trip from happening if not organized in advance. They include money, passports, visas, vaccinations, tickets, and insurance.

> THE **TIME TO MINIMIZE** THE CHANCES OF AN **'IF ONLY'** SITUATION IS DURING THE **PLANNING STAGE**.

YOUR TEAM

If you're planning a trip with a group, remember that team dynamics play a very important role in the trip's success. When planning a long trip, it's a good idea to plan shorter trips beforehand, as practice sessions, in terms of both equipment and group dynamics, to help you organize your team more effectively in the future.

MIXED-GENDER GROUPS

If the team has both male and female members, remember to factor this into the planning stage. You'll need to consider arrangements for sleeping and washing, who carries what, who is responsible for what, and so on. Assuming that the women will cook while the men make the shelters is not the best way to start a trip.

Preparation through training

It's important to train yourself mentally and physically, and practice with the equipment you'll be using. You'll get the most out of your trip if you're prepared to a level that means you can operate within your capabilities. This will allow you to enjoy and appreciate the experience.

TRAINING WITH EQUIPMENT
Find out the best way to operate your equipment by practicing under realistic conditions (see box, below). This will highlight its strengths and weaknesses, as well as your own. Before you set off, think about the skills required, and ensure that you're capable of addressing those demands.

REALISTIC TRAINING

When training with new equipment, practice using it in realistic conditions. For example, if you'll be using your GPS in the cold, are you able to operate it with the gloves you have? If pitching a tent, do you have all the required components, and can you put it up in the dark and rain?

TRAINING YOURSELF

Duplicate in training what you intend to do on your trip. Build up your training gradually, and take into account the following:

The environment	Research the weather conditions you'll be facing, and look at the extremes and the average. For example, desert areas may be hot during the day, but can drop to below-freezing at night.
Weight	Increase the amount of weight you carry until you're eventually carrying what you intend to take. This will not only condition you to the weight, but will also help you decide what's important to take.
Distance	If your trip involves covering a certain distance a day, train for that distance. This will give you an indication of whether it's achievable and sustainable.
Language	If you're visiting a country in which your native language is not widely spoken, try to learn some useful phrases. Take a phrase book or an electronic translator.

Emergency plan of action

Even the most meticulously planned trip can run into difficulties. Unforecast strong winds could trap you and your kayak on an island overnight, or a sprained ankle could leave you unable to climb down rocks. These scenarios are difficult to predict, but could easily happen.

Running into problems

There are two sides to any survival or rescue situation: the part you play and the part the rescue services play. Rescue services are more effective if they have all the relevant information. Keep people informed of your intended whereabouts, so they can raise the alarm if you deviate from your plans.

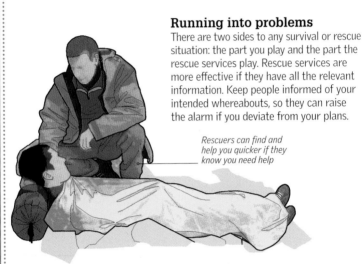

Rescuers can find and help you quicker if they know you need help

Keeping people informed

Write down your trip details, including pertinent itinerary places and dates. Prepare an "emergency plan of action" (EPA, see opposite). Give a copy to your next of kin and group members, and keep a copy yourself. Where applicable, inform local services, such as park and ranger stations, of your plans.

WRITING AN EMERGENCY PLAN OF ACTION (EPA)

Consider your worst-case scenario (see box, below), and see what information people would need about you. If you did go missing, especially in another country, rescue services would need a recent photograph, passport details, the equipment you are carrying, and the languages you speak.

WORST-CASE SCENARIO

In the military, every mission that's undertaken, particularly in a theater of conflict, has plans for the worst-case scenario. Each part of the mission is meticulously planned, and the team completes a form that states what their basic intention will be if anything happens during the various stages.

IF THE WORST HAPPENS

Should the team find themselves in difficulty, the rescue group will have a clear indication of the team's intent and can plan effectively around this information. The team will be found quicker as a result of this. It is a good idea to apply this principle to your own trip.

EMERGENCY PLAN OF ACTION FORM

Full name as on passport:
John William Smith

Date of birth:
(mm/dd/yy)
05/28/60

Height:
5' 10" (178cm)
Weight: 168 lbs (76 kilos)

Hair color:
Brown

Passport number:
208XXXX63
Expires:
11/03/13

Driver's license number:
744 988 440
Expires:
12/28/15

Distinguishing marks (scars, tattoos):
Large scar—right hand, middle finger
Small scar—center of forehead
Chinese symbol tattoo—right arm

Languages spoken (fluent/basic):
English—native
French—basic
German—basic

Medication:
Anti-malaria tablets

Allergies:
Amoxicillin

Swimmer: Strong swimmer
Outdoor skills/experience:
Attended basic military survival training.
Attended basic bushcraft course
Experienced in living outdoors

Next of kin 1: Father
William Smith
1018 Furlong Avenue
Brunswick, Maine,
USA 04555

Next of kin 2: Brother
Andrew Smith
1023 Parkglen
Ashford, Kent,
TM24 5HZ, UK

Tel: (001) 55 555 2356

Tel: (0044) (0)155 555 2357

Email: willsmith@internet.com

Email: andrewsmith@internet.com

Trip details:
Campsite 1 = Grid ST456654
Campsite 2 = Grid ST654987
Vehicles: Landrover 1 = white, reg MH55 555
　　　　　Landrover 2 = blue, reg MH56 555
Group = Ben Jones, Kim Smith, and myself
Day 1: Park Landrover 2 at Campsite 2, and drive in Landrover 1 to Campsite 1
Day 2: Follow well-defined path along the Derwent Line Trail, aiming to camp overnight at Grid 4561559
Day 3: Continue along the Derwent Line Trail, aiming to be at Campsite 2 by midafternoon. Camp overnight at Campsite 2

Day 4: Travel in Landrover 2 to campsite 1 and retrieve Landrover 1

Foreseeable problems/intentions:
Day 1: None
Day 2: None, but will use Ranger Station 18, grid 555555 (Tel. 666 6666) as an emergency rendezvous point
Day 3: None, but will use Ranger Station 19, grid 666666 (Tel. 555 5555) as an emergency rendezvous point
Day 4: None

Communications plan:
Will speak to Dad on the morning of Day 1 and try to phone during the trek, but am unsure of cell reception once on the trail, so don't worry if you hear nothing. Will phone Dad again when we reach campsite 2 on Day 3.

My cell: 07979 555555
My email: jws@internet.com
Alt. No: Ben 05555 555555
Alt. No: Kim 05555 555555
Alt. No: Campsite 1 555 555 55555
Alt. No: Campsite 2 555 555 55555

Date: March 23, 2011

Understanding your environment

Before you head off into the wilderness, it is important to fully prepare for the environment. Research how the native inhabitants dress, work, and eat. Knowing how they have adapted to their way of life will help you understand the environment and allow you to select the best gear and equipment, adopt the best techniques, and learn the correct skills. This is crucial, given that most survival situations arise due to a sequence of events that could have been easily avoided.

> " YOUR BODY NEEDS **WATER TO DIGEST FOOD**, SO ALWAYS **PRIORITIZE WATER OVER FOOD**. "

The four basic principles of survival

Protection, location, water, and food are the basic principles of survival. In most survival situations, this is also the order in which you should prioritize them.

PROTECTION

You must stay in a condition that allows you to be proactive in your continued survival and rescue. Physically, protect yourself against injury, the elements, and wildlife. Mentally, guard yourself against emotions that could rob you of the will to live: fear, guilt, and depression, for example. The best way to achieve this is to light and maintain a fire. Not only does it offer physical protection, but it also provides a sense of security and familiarity that can help normalize even the most dire situation.

WATER

You should understand how a lack of water affects you and learn how to procure water in your environment. While you may be able to survive for a few days without it, your ability to perform even simple mental and physical tasks will be dramatically reduced in less than 24 hours. However, if you're injured, if the weather conditions are hot, and if your workload is quite heavy, your survival time without water could be reduced to a few hours.

LOCATION

Recognize the importance of your location to your chances of survival and rescue. You will usually have two options: stay or go. Your preferred option should be to remain where you are and use anything at your disposal to mark your location to help rescuers find you. If you can't stay where you are (perhaps due to imminent danger), you may have to move to another location that provides either a better chance of survival or rescue, or both. Select a location aid that offers you the best chance of attracting attention.

FOOD

The importance of food is directly related to the length of time you are in a survival situation: the longer the situation lasts, the more crucial food will become in helping you stay fit. Even with a moderate workload, going without food for five to seven days will not kill you. You will, of course, feel hungry, grow tired, your movements will slow, and your body will lose its ability to repair itself. However, unless you are malnourished before you enter a survival situation, you're unlikely to starve to death within a week.

Surviving in temperate areas

Most temperate environments have a mild climate and good natural resources, making them favorable places for long-term survival. The abundance of rain means that rivers and lakes are common, and swampy wetlands form in areas with poor drainage. Potentially the greatest threat is hypothermia, especially in winter and at night.

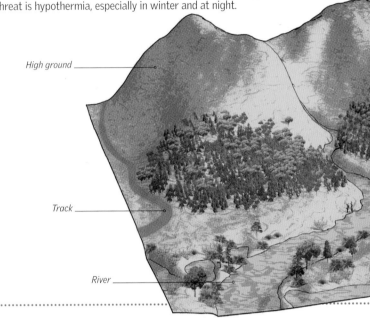

High ground

Track

River

Surviving in the rainforest

While natural resources are abundant here, heat, humidity, animals, and voracious vegetal growth can make it uncomfortable. Mosquitoes can cause more fatalities than any other creature. Identification of edible plants is crucial to avoid poisonous species. The greatest danger is getting lost, since dense undergrowth makes navigation difficult.

TROPICAL ESSENTIALS

Rainforests contain everything you need for survival, but remember the following when venturing out:

- Most animals in the jungle want to avoid you as much as you want to avoid them—making a noise will scare most away.
- Boil or treat all water.
- High humidity encourages infections, so keep yourself covered, and wash whenever possible.
- Always build shelters and sleep off the ground.
- Dry tinder is hard to find, so if you find any, keep it dry.
- Rivers in the jungle usually run downhill to civilization, and eventually to the coast.

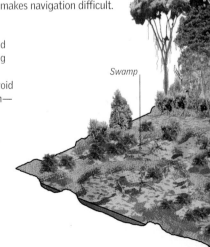

Swamp

TEMPERATE ESSENTIALS

Climate and terrain can vary widely, so prepare for a range of eventualities:

• Weather can change quickly, so check the local forecast before you set off, and carry an AM/FM radio to listen to local weather reports.

• Plan a realistic route, and prepare an EPA (see pp.18–19). Be ready to reassess your route during the trip.

• Take clothing for all possible conditions.

• Carry a survival can (see pp.34–35), knife, emergency equipment, cell phone, and first-aid kit (see pp.166–69), and learn how to use them.

• Carry adequate water, and the equipment to purify more if needed.

• Carry some form of basic shelter, even if only going out for the day.

• Take a map and compass, and consider using a GPS as an aid.

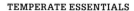

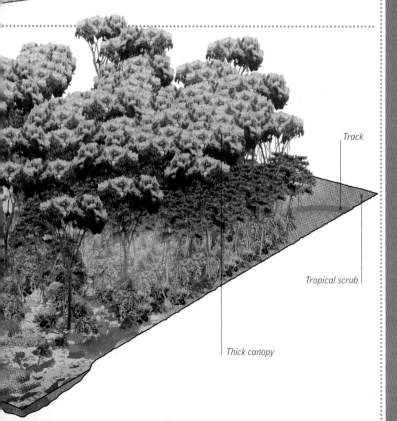

Woodland

Open ground

Track

Tropical scrub

Thick canopy

Surviving in the cold

In cold environments natural resources may be scarce, so your survival is likely to depend on your equipment and supplies. Shelters can be dug from the snow, but fire essentials are limited in polar and tundra areas. The greatest dangers are hypothermia and—in northern areas—polar bears. Survival is more feasible in the taiga, where wood, fresh water, and edible flora and fauna are available.

COLD ESSENTIALS

The main threats in cold environments are hypothermia and exposure, so ensure you are fully prepared:

• Dress in loose-fitting layers of clothing (see pp.30–31), avoid overheating, and make sure that your clothing stays dry and clean.

• If your hands are cold, warming them with your breath will make them wet; instead, tuck them under your armpits.

• Get off the ground, snow, or ice—sit on your pack or make a sleeping platform using boughs to avoid losing body heat.

• Regularly check your extremities (face, toes, hands, and ears) for frost nip, the first stage of frostbite.

• Wind-chill is dangerous, so take shelter from the wind at every chance, particularly if you are in a survival situation.

• Ensure your shelter is ventilated—keep vent holes clear and check them, especially during heavy snowfalls.

• If fire is your primary means of warmth, triple the amount of firewood you think you need—you will need enough to last the night.

Surviving in the desert

Hostile temperatures and few natural resources limit chances of survival in the desert. Water and shelter are scarce, so the greatest dangers are dehydration and heat exhaustion, although African savanna areas may be home to dangerous mammals. Desert areas are home to a range of venomous snakes.

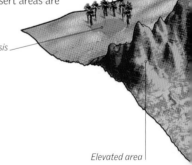

Oasis

Elevated area

DESERT ESSENTIALS

Survival in the extreme conditions of the desert is impossible without full preparation. Consider the following:

• Always prepare an EPA (see pp.18–19) to notify someone of your plans before entering a desert area.

• Carry extra water, and carry equipment to maximize your chances of procuring more.

• If your vehicle breaks down, leave it only if staying is no longer safe or feasible.

• If venturing into remote areas, augment your map and compass with a GPS, and consider taking a PLB or satellite phone (see pp.158–59).

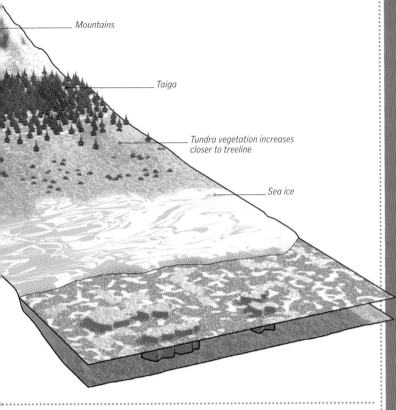

Mountains

Taiga

Tundra vegetation increases
closer to treeline

Sea ice

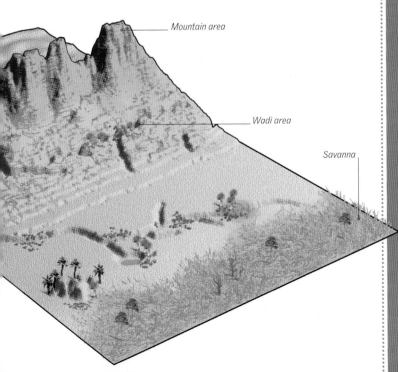

Mountain area

Wadi area

Savanna

Surviving in the mountains

The prospects for survival are good at lower elevations, where trees, rivers, and edible plants and animals are likely to be present. At higher elevations, there are fewer resources, and the risk of avalanches and crevasses, and cold-related injuries, pose the greatest threat.

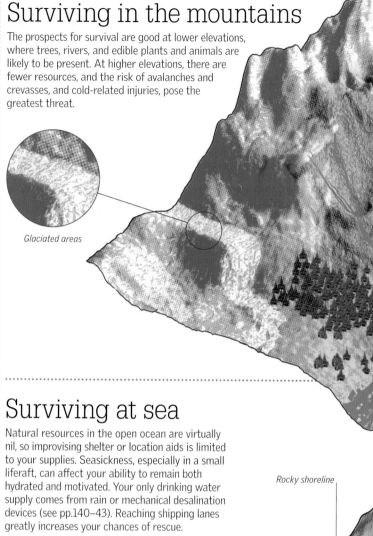

Glaciated areas

Surviving at sea

Natural resources in the open ocean are virtually nil, so improvising shelter or location aids is limited to your supplies. Seasickness, especially in a small liferaft, can affect your ability to remain both hydrated and motivated. Your only drinking water supply comes from rain or mechanical desalination devices (see pp.140–43). Reaching shipping lanes greatly increases your chances of rescue.

MARINE ESSENTIALS
Consider the following to increase your chances of survival at sea:
• Pack sea-survival equipment as if your life depends on it—it might!
• Take emergency immersion-survival suits to protect yourself and aid floatation and location.
• Always carry a Personal Locator Beacon (PLB).
• Take several means of obtaining water (see pp.140–43).
• Don't abandon your vessel until absolutely necessary.
• Take anti-seasickness tablets.

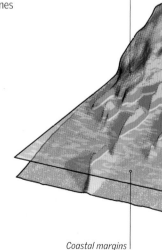

Rocky shoreline

Coastal margins

Avalanche-prone slopes

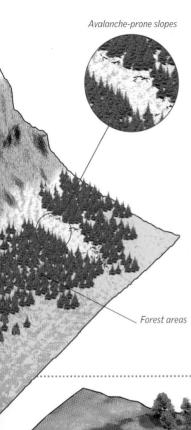

Forest areas

MOUNTAIN ESSENTIALS

High altitude and lower oxygen levels place higher-than-normal demands on your body and equipment.

• Respect nature and err on the side of caution—rescue is unlikely to be quick or easy on a mountain.

• Plan an achievable route, and prepare an EPA (see pp.18–19).

• Dress in layers. Start a walk lightly dressed (cold) and add or remove layers as necessary.

• Wear a hat and gloves.

• Take a flashlight—weather changes and unforeseen problems may mean you are on the mountain in darkness.

• Carry an avalanche transceiver.

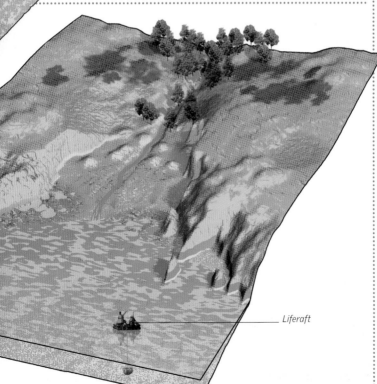

Liferaft

Choosing your gear

Forward planning is essential when deciding what equipment to take on your trip. Assess your personal requirements, the likely weather and terrain, and the amount of gear you'll be able to transport.

Packing for your trip

Weigh up your particular gear requirements against the limitations of your chosen mode of transportation. Organize and prioritize your gear (see opposite) so that any items you may need in a survival scenario are always close at hand.

HOW MUCH TO PACK

The environment of the region you're traveling to will dictate the type of equipment you will need to take with you, but your proposed mode of transportation is the main constraint on the quantity of gear. Additional weight will make traveling uncomfortable, use up too much valuable energy, slow your progress, and limit the distance you can travel each day.

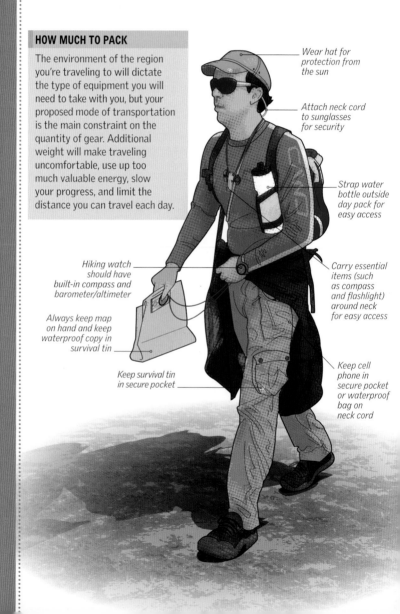

Wear hat for protection from the sun

Attach neck cord to sunglasses for security

Strap water bottle outside day pack for easy access

Hiking watch should have built-in compass and barometer/altimeter

Always keep map on hand and keep waterproof copy in survival tin

Keep survival tin in secure pocket

Carry essential items (such as compass and flashlight) around neck for easy access

Keep cell phone in secure pocket or waterproof bag on neck cord

Prioritizing your gear

Irrespective of how much gear you decide to take, you should organize individual items into three categories—first-line, second-line, and third-line—according to their importance to your survival. This way, in an emergency you'll have all your essential items on your person, or close enough to grab at a second's notice.

FIRST-LINE GEAR

This is your basic survival equipment. If something goes wrong and you have to abandon the bulk of your gear, what you're standing in is all you'll have to help you survive. This includes crucial items of outdoor clothing and essential items for navigation and safety. Your bushcraft knife, firesteel, and belt pouch make up your belt order (see p.35). You will need to risk-assess your situation and adapt your gear priorities accordingly, as conditions change.

SECOND-LINE GEAR

This includes all you would need to stay safe under normal conditions. The idea is that you carry it at all times. Examples of second-line gear include:
- A spare set of clothes, a bivi sack, and cordage
- Emergency rations and first-aid kit (see pp.166–69)
- A hexamine stove and items to make a hot drink
- A matchless fireset and metal cup

THIRD-LINE GEAR

Also known as your "sustainment load," third-line gear is essentially the equipment you need to keep yourself alive and to function for longer periods of time. How much third-line gear you have will ultimately depend on your mode of transportation and the amount of equipment you can carry. Examples of third-line gear include:
- A form of shelter—a tent or a tarpaulin
- Cooking utensils, such as a stove or cooking pot
- A backpack
- Food stores
- A sleeping bag and sleeping mat
- Any large water containers or hydration packs
- A wash kit and sanitary items

PACK YOUR GEAR IN **REVERSE ORDER**: THE THINGS YOU'LL **NEED FIRST** SHOULD BE THE **LAST THINGS YOU PACK**.

Dressing for the outdoors

Modern outdoor clothing is highly sophisticated and technologically advanced. Materials and designs are lightweight, hard-wearing, and versatile. Choose fabrics and combinations most suited to the environment and conditions in which you are traveling.

REGULATING BODY HEAT

Don't be tempted to overdress. Sweat can soak you as much as rain, and a sudden change of temperature can cause hypothermia. Wear layers to control your body temperature.

Layering clothes

Several light layers are better than one heavy layer. Wearing multiple layers gives you flexibility to fine-tune your temperature by taking off or putting on layers. Wool, fleece, microfleece, and down are good insulators.

How layering works

Layering traps air between the layers and helps you stay warm in any environment. Wearing the correct layers in the right order is important. Wear wicking fabrics, such as polypropylene, in hot and cold weather.

THE LAYERING SYSTEM

The outer layer repels rain, while dampness is wicked away by the base layer. The mid-layers insulate the body.

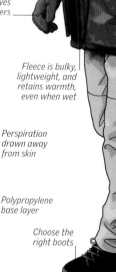

Wear hat to prevent excessive loss of body heat through head

Base layer wicks moisture away from skin

Outer layer prevents moisture from entering while allowing sweat to escape

Mid-layer provides warmth

Fleece gloves worn under lightweight gloves help protect fingers

Fleece is bulky, lightweight, and retains warmth, even when wet

Breathable outer layer repels rain

Perspiration drawn away from skin

Polypropylene base layer

Choose the right boots

Lightweight, full-length pants shade skin from the Sun

Skin *Fleece mid-layer* *Synthetic mesh*

Footwear

When deciding on your footwear, first think of your personal needs, including the shape of your feet and the support you need. Also consider the distance and terrain you'll be covering, and the cost. When you buy a pair of boots, wear them around the house and go on short hikes to make sure you have broken them in.

Flexible, breathable fabric upper dries quickly

Shock-absorbing sole

LIGHTWEIGHT BOOT
Fabric and leather hybrids combine the support and traction of a heavier shoe with the flexibility of a sports shoe.

Padded ankle gives comfort and support

Sole provides good grip

HIKING BOOTS
Combining weight, durability, and protection produces a good, all-around leather boot with water-resistant uppers.

High uppers keep mud off your pants

Canvas uppers designed to keep feet cool

Wide, deep studs aid grip

JUNGLE-TREKKING BOOT
Made of rot-proof leather and canvas, this has a directly molded sole. Holes in the instep aid ventilation and drain moisture.

ANATOMY OF A SOLE
A boot sole has many layers. Look for a good tread on the outsole, and cushioning under the heel and toe.

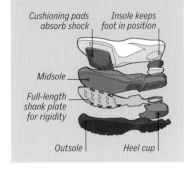

Cushioning pads absorb shock

Insole keeps foot in position

Midsole

Full-length shank plate for rigidity

Outsole

Heel cup

PACKING A BACKPACK
Always pack in reverse order: the items you need first should go in last. Heavy items should be placed close to your back to prevent the pack from pulling away from your shoulders.

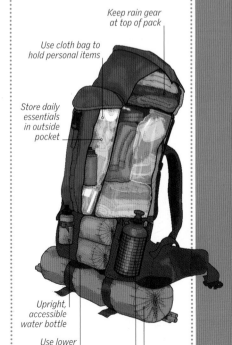

Keep rain gear at top of pack

Use cloth bag to hold personal items

Store daily essentials in outside pocket

Upright, accessible water bottle

Use lower compartment for sleeping bag and mat

Extra water on outside of pack

Strap tent to bottom of pack

Extreme survival: in the wilderness

WHAT TO DO

ARE YOU IN DANGER?

If you are in a group, try to help any others who are in danger

 NO YES ▶

Get yourself out of it:
Elements—Find or improvise shelter immediately
Animals—Avoid confrontation
Injury—Stabilize condition and apply first aid

▶ **ASSESS YOUR SITUATION** ◀
See pp.154–157

▼

DOES ANYONE KNOW YOU ARE MISSING OR WHERE YOU ARE?

If no one knows you are missing or where you are, you must notify people of your plight by any means

◀ NO YES ▶

If you are missed, a rescue party will almost certainly be despatched to find you

▼

DO YOU HAVE ANY MEANS OF COMMUNICATION?

You're faced with surviving for an indefinite period—until you are located or you find help

◀ NO YES ▶

If you have a cell or satellite phone, let someone know your predicament. If your situation calls for an emergency rescue, and you have a Personal Locator Beacon (PLB), consider this option

▼

CAN YOU SURVIVE WHERE YOU ARE? *

If you cannot survive where you are and there are no physical reasons why you should remain, move to a location that offers a better chance of survival, rescue, or both

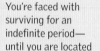 NO YES ▶

Address the Principles of Survival: Protection; Location; Water; Food

▼ ▼

YOU WILL HAVE TO MOVE **

YOU SHOULD STAY **

YOU WILL HAVE TO MOVE **

 YOU SHOULD STAY **

▼ ▼

DO

- Find an elevated position from which to choose a suitable area for survival and rescue
- Regulate your clothing to avoid overheating when moving and hypothermia when static
- Use or improvise a walking stick to help reduce trips and falls
- Improvise shelter when not moving
- Plan your route around potential or known water sources. Filter and purify all water where possible
- Have location aids accessible while moving and deployed when static

DO

- Check your shelter site, before building, for hazards such as insects, flooding, rock falls, wild animals, and deadfalls
- Inventory and ration your supplies
- Keep a fire going; you can use it to purify water, keep warm, and signal rescue
- Fill plastic bags or spare clothing with dry foliage and use them as a mattress or pillow to insulate you from the cold or damp ground
- If in a group, give everyone something to do to keep them occupied and lessen their worry

DON'T

- Ignore your fire—be on a constant lookout for dry tinder/kindling and fuel
- Walk faster than the pace of the slowest person in your group
- Be careless when walking downhill—a twisted ankle could prove fatal
- Under or overdress. Start off a walk lightly dressed and add or remove layers as necessary

DON'T

- Leave food in your campsite as it will be at risk from predators
- Shelter too deep in the woods despite the protection it gives you from elements. Remember: your location aids need to be seen
- Eat unidentified food, since it could worsen your situation through illness. Food is not a priority in a short-term situation

* If you cannot survive where you are, but you also cannot move because of injury or other factors, you must do everything you can to attract rescue.

** If your situation changes (for instance, you are "moving" to find help, and you find a suitable location in which you can stay and survive) consult the alternative "Dos" and "Don'ts."

Your survival kit

A basic survival kit is an essential item to take with you on any outdoor expedition. It should be compact enough to carry at all times, and its contents should address the key principles of survival: protection, location, water, and food.

Preparing your survival kit

Choose a tin with a waterproof seal and locking clasps. While you can buy ready-made kits, you should always adapt the contents to your needs and to the environment you'll be in. Items in your kit should be high-quality and multi-purpose. Your kit should contain the following:

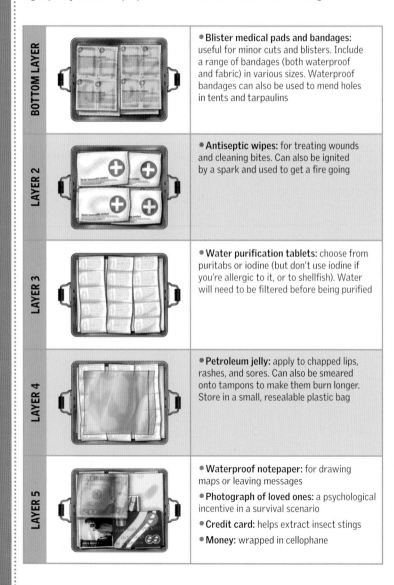

BOTTOM LAYER	● **Blister medical pads and bandages:** useful for minor cuts and blisters. Include a range of bandages (both waterproof and fabric) in various sizes. Waterproof bandages can also be used to mend holes in tents and tarpaulins
LAYER 2	● **Antiseptic wipes:** for treating wounds and cleaning bites. Can also be ignited by a spark and used to get a fire going
LAYER 3	● **Water purification tablets:** choose from puritabs or iodine (but don't use iodine if you're allergic to it, or to shellfish). Water will need to be filtered before being purified
LAYER 4	● **Petroleum jelly:** apply to chapped lips, rashes, and sores. Can also be smeared onto tampons to make them burn longer. Store in a small, resealable plastic bag
LAYER 5	● **Waterproof notepaper:** for drawing maps or leaving messages ● **Photograph of loved ones:** a psychological incentive in a survival scenario ● **Credit card:** helps extract insect stings ● **Money:** wrapped in cellophane

ADDITIONAL USEFUL ITEMS

While your survival tin's size may be restrictive, you can fit items in your "belt order." This will form part of your first-line equipment (see p.29).

• **Space blanket or aluminum foil:** use as a signaling device; for shelter; to carry water; or to cook in. Many are dual-sided: one silver, the other green for camouflage, or orange to stand out
• **Plastic bags:** have many uses, from a water carrier to a transpiration bag

• **Medicines (such as painkillers and antibiotics):** so you have the basics if you're separated from your gear
• **Small candle:** provides a reliable flame to build your fire around
• **Nylon tights:** for warmth, or as an improvised water filter, mosquito net, or fishing net
• **Small AM/FM radio:** battery or solar-powered
• **Surgical tubing:** to procure water
• **Fire can/matchless fireset:** self-contained methods of starting a fire

LAYER 6		• **Survival saw, or pocket chainsaw:** can be wrapped around the inside of the tin or cut in half, if space is limited • **Single-edged razor:** multi-purpose tool • **Needle and thread:** use strong, waxed cotton, pre-threaded through the needle
LAYER 7		• **Flashlights:** small white and red Photon lights—taped in "off" position • **Mini multi-tool:** includes useful features, such as a compass and saw • **High-viz card, signal mirror:** location aids • **Compass:** an emergency back-up • **Flint, fire steel, tampons:** for starting fires
LAYER 8		• **Waterproof matches and tinder balls:** for starting fires. Store the matches in a small, resealable plastic bag • **Pencil:** sharpened at both ends • **Potassium permanganate:** dissolve in water to sterilize water, and to clean wounds, and to make fire
LAYER 9		• **Non-lubricated condoms:** can be used to carry water, or as a waterproof cover for smaller items, such as your cell phone • **Mini fishing kit:** useful if you're near water. Fishing line can be used for other tasks, also. Should contain a selection of hooks, flies, swivels, and split-shots
SEALED TIN LID		• **Sailmaker's needles:** multi-purpose—can be used as an arrow point, or for mending tents and tarpaulins. Wide eyes are best • **Safety pins:** for securing clothing, or mending your sleeping bag or tent • **Mini glowsticks (cyalumes):** useful for emergency lighting, and as a location aid

On the Trail

On the Trail

Before you set off on an expedition, you should have at least a basic understanding of how to read a map and use a compass. Your ability to correctly assess a map of the area you intend to visit will allow you to make informed decisions while preparing for your trip. If you understand the area and terrain, your chances of getting lost will be reduced, and you will be able to evaluate continually your progress and therefore alter your plans as necessary.

You will also be able to plan the safest and most appropriate route, and locate water, shelter, and areas that will allow you to use your location aids properly. If you're proficient with a map and compass, you'll have no cause to worry about getting lost or straying off-track and will be free to enjoy your outdoors experience.

In a survival situation, you will be faced with many tough decisions. You may have to decide whether to stay where you are and await rescue or move to an area that offers a better chance of survival and rescue. Your ability to navigate effectively—whether by using a map and compass or by using natural features—will play a major role in your decision-making process. While a Global Positioning System (GPS) is an excellent aid, it relies on batteries and technology—both of which can fail.

Before you venture into an unfamiliar environment, carefully research the type of terrain you will be encountering, and investigate the best method of traveling safely and efficiently across it. Simply checking the weather forecast before you go will also allow you to evaluate conditions and make informed decisions before you travel. The ability to assess your situation and modify your plans means that you will be able to avoid many potential survival situations.

❝ IF YOU ARE ABLE TO **UNDERSTAND THE AREA** AND TERRAIN, YOUR CHANCES OF **GETTING LOST WILL BE REDUCED**. **❞**

Walking on set bearings

The ability to take a bearing (see pp.44–47) and navigate using pace counting (see p.48) could prove to be crucial skills in a survival situation.

Test how accurately you can walk on a set bearing and pace out a set distance by following the exercise below. If you have stayed on your bearings and your pacing has been accurate, you should finish at your starting point. Pick a suitable area where you can walk at least 330ft (100m) in any direction. Don't cheat by heading for your marker!

1 Place a marker on the ground. Dial a bearing onto your compass (110° in our example).

2 Walk on the bearing, counting your paces until you think you've traveled 330ft (100m), then stop.

3 Add 120° to your original bearing. Dial this new bearing (230° in our example) onto your compass.

4 Pace out another 330ft (100m) on your new bearing, then stop.

5 Add another 120° to the latest bearing. Dial a last bearing (350° in our example) onto your compass.

6 Walk on your final bearing for another 330ft (100m). You should be back at your starting point.

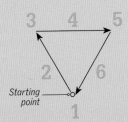

Starting point

Maps and map-reading

A **map is a two-dimensional** representation of a three-dimensional area—from it, you can determine distance and height on the ground. If you can interpret a map, you can visualize what an area looks like and use these features to make navigation easier.

The legend

Topographic maps include a legend, or key, to decipher the information shown on the map. This helps you visualize what's being shown. Some examples include:

HEIGHTS AND NATURAL FEATURES

WATER   MUD

VERTICAL FACE/CLIFF

BOULDERS   OUTCROP

VEGETATION

BRACKEN, HEATH, ROUGH GRASSLAND

CONIFEROUS TREES

NON-CONIFEROUS TREES

THE SCALE

Hiking maps are drawn to a scale given in the legend. This is a ratio of how much you would have to enlarge the map to reach actual size. 1:25,000, where 4cm on a map equates to 1km on the ground (2$\frac{1}{2}$ in to 1 mile), is the most useful level of detail for hikers. A smaller scale of, say, 1:50,00 will give a more basic overview of the terrain.

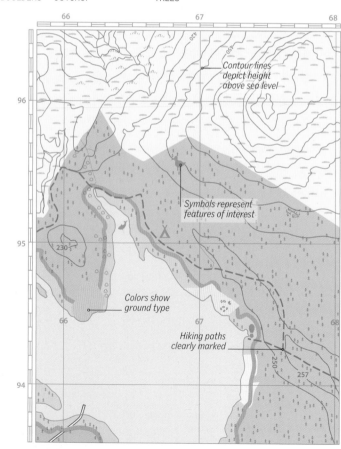

Contour lines depict height above sea level

Symbols represent features of interest

Colors show ground type

Hiking paths clearly marked

Measuring distance

Maps are drawn to scale so you can use them to estimate distances on the ground accurately. This makes it possible to work out the most direct and energy-efficient route to your destination. Some methods include:

USING THE GRID LINES
On a scale 1:25,000 map, each grid square shows 1km (if traveling diagonally across a square, it's about 1.5km). You can also lay a piece of paper between the two points, mark the start and end of your route, and measure it against the scale line.

USING STRING OR SOLDER
If navigating around obstacles or bends, curve a piece of string around your intended route and transfer it to the scale line. Solder wire (use lead-free wire) is even more accurate, since it holds its shape on the map and stays flexible.

Contour lines

A contour line joins points of equal height above sea level, and allows the ground's topography to be shown in detail. The contour interval is given in the legend—for scale 1:25,000 maps, you would usually see a 5-m vertical interval between each line, but for mountain maps, it may be 10m.

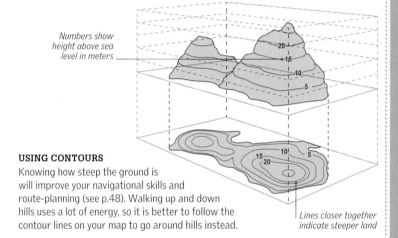

Numbers show height above sea level in meters

USING CONTOURS
Knowing how steep the ground is will improve your navigational skills and route-planning (see p.48). Walking up and down hills uses a lot of energy, so it is better to follow the contour lines on your map to go around hills instead.

Lines closer together indicate steeper land

Grid references

Grid lines help you locate a specific point, using a unique number called a grid reference. Vertical lines are called "eastings," since their value increases as they travel east on the map. Horizontal lines are called "northings."

WORKING OUT GRID REFERENCES
Using the numbers on the grid lines, apply the easting number first. On a scale 1:25,000 map, the shaded area (right) would have a reference of 2046, showing a 1km by 1km square. To be more accurate, use a six-figure number—mentally divide the square into tenths. The cross would then have a reference of 185445.

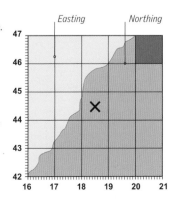

Get your bearings

In addition to being able to read a map, you should know how to orientate your map to the land so you can use it to navigate. The most reliable way to do this is with a compass. Use a compass to determine direction, orientate your map and yourself, take and plot bearings, and navigate.

How a compass works

A compass needle is a magnetized piece of metal that, when allowed to rotate freely, will orientate itself to the North and South magnetic poles.

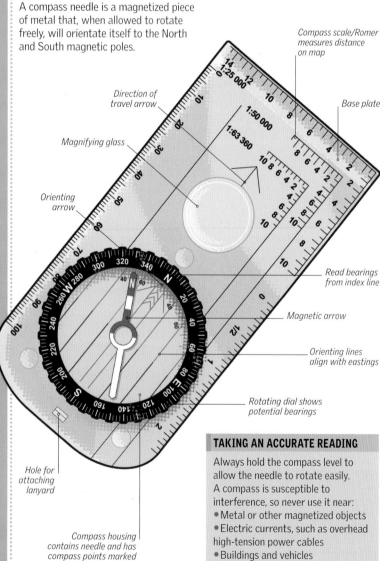

Compass scale/Romer measures distance on map

Direction of travel arrow

Base plate

Magnifying glass

Orienting arrow

Read bearings from index line

Magnetic arrow

Orienting lines align with eastings

Rotating dial shows potential bearings

Hole for attaching lanyard

Compass housing contains needle and has compass points marked on circular, rotating bezel

TAKING AN ACCURATE READING

Always hold the compass level to allow the needle to rotate easily. A compass is susceptible to interference, so never use it near:
- Metal or other magnetized objects
- Electric currents, such as overhead high-tension power cables
- Buildings and vehicles

Setting your map

Walking with your map set allows you to read the ground from the map as you pass over it, and to recognize and predict features as you progress, which means that you'll soon realize if you are heading off course.

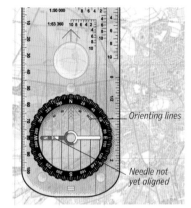

Orienting lines

Needle not yet aligned

1 Rotate the dial so that "N" sits under the index line. Lay your map flat on the ground and ensure there is nothing nearby that could affect your compass (see box, opposite). Lay the compass on the map so its edge runs parallel with a vertical grid line (easting).

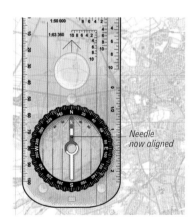

Needle now aligned

2 Keeping the orienting lines aligned with the grid lines on the map, rotate the entire map until the north magnetic needle on the compass sits inside the orienting arrow. The map is now set to magnetic north and should line up with the features around you.
• If the magnetic variation in your area is higher than 5°, compensate accordingly (see panel, right).

MAGNETIC VARIATION

Map legends refer to north in three ways: "true north," "grid north," and "magnetic north." The angle between magnetic north and grid north is called "magnetic variation," and is given in the map legend. True north is the direction of a meridian of longitude that converges on the North Pole. Grid north runs parallel to the vertical grid lines on a map, and differs from true north since a map is flat. Magnetic north is the direction indicated by a magnetic compass.

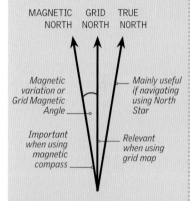

MAGNETIC NORTH   GRID NORTH   TRUE NORTH

Magnetic variation or Grid Magnetic Angle

Important when using magnetic compass

Mainly useful if navigating using North Star

Relevant when using grid map

COMPENSATING FOR VARIATION

When converting a magnetic bearing to a grid bearing, or vice versa, you have to adjust for magnetic variation. When the variation is west, use the phrases "Mag to grid—get rid" or "Grid to mag—add." If the variation is east, the opposite applies.

1 Check the legend of your map to establish the magnetic variation. This depends on your location, and whether it is east or west of grid north.

2 If the variation is 0°, there's no magnetic variation affecting the compass, so make no adjustments.

3 If converting a magnetic bearing to a grid bearing with a 12° west variation, take off the 12°. With an east variation, add it on.

4 If converting a grid bearing to a magnetic bearing with a 12° west variation, add on the 12°. With an east variation, take it off.

Taking bearings using a map

Always give any compass work your full attention. Rushing it, especially when working out bearings, can lead to navigational errors that could get you lost. Using your map to navigate is simple. Use your compass as a protractor to work out your bearing, and then to keep you on track.

> ❝ **NEVER UNDERESTIMATE** THE COMBINED POWER OF A **MAP**, **COMPASS**, AND THE SKILLS AND KNOWLEDGE TO USE THEM WELL – YOUR **LIFE MAY DEPEND ON IT**. ❞

BACK BEARING

This enables you to find your position by taking a bearing from a feature back to you. Take a bearing to a point in the normal way and either add or subtract 180 degrees. You can also read the bearing exactly opposite to the index line. This is useful when working out the bearing from a feature back to you and transferring it to your map (see p.46).

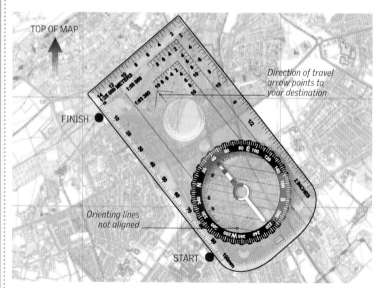

TOP OF MAP

FINISH

Direction of travel arrow points to your destination

Orienting lines not aligned

START

1 Lay your map on a flat surface and ensure that nothing nearby interferes with the compass reading (see box, p.42).
• Lay the edge of your compass so that it runs between the point you want to navigate from and the point you want to navigate toward.

2 Make sure that the direction of travel arrow on the compass is pointing in the direction that you want to travel in on the map.

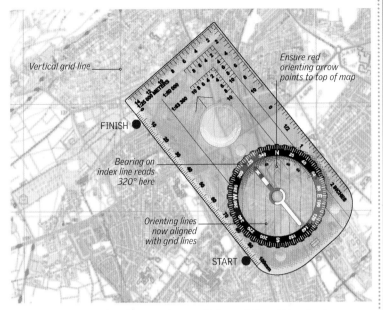

Vertical grid line

Ensure red orienting arrow points to top of map

FINISH

Bearing on index line reads 320° here

Orienting lines now aligned with grid lines

START

3 Turn the compass housing around until the orienting arrow and the orienting lines line up with the vertical grid lines on the map. Read the bearing between the two points from the index line on the compass.

4 Convert the grid bearing to a magnetic bearing by using the magnetic variation information on the map legend (see p.43). Add or subtract your figure, and adjust your compass accordingly.

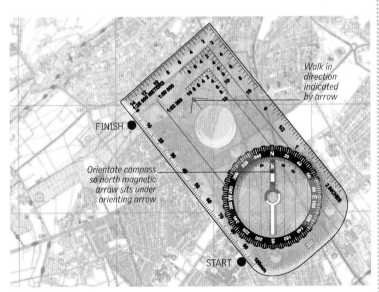

FINISH

Walk in direction indicated by arrow

Orientate compass so north magnetic arrow sits under orienting arrow

START

5 In order to walk on this bearing, you must now orientate your compass.
• Hold the compass level and at a height that allows you to comfortably look squarely down on it (close to your chest is a good position).

6 Turn your body until the north end of the compass needle sits inside the orienting arrow. The direction of travel arrow is now pointing exactly in the direction in which you need to walk.

Taking bearings using features on the ground

You may need to take a bearing to a specific point to navigate toward it. The point may be a feature you can see at the time but could lose sight of during your journey because of the terrain. You can also plot bearings on a map to work out your own position (see below and opposite).

Point direction
of travel arrow
at feature

Ensure map and
compass are level

TAKING A BEARING ON A FEATURE
Pointing your compass at the feature, hold
the base plate steady and rotate the compass
housing until the orienting arrow sits directly
under the north needle. This is the magnetic
bearing you would use to navigate to the feature.

Transferring bearings onto a map

You must know how to transfer a compass bearing from a feature (a magnetic bearing) onto a map (a grid bearing). For this example, imagine that the magnetic variation is 12° west. Take a bearing on your chosen feature (see above). Here it is 45° magnetic. You would subtract the magnetic variation (12°) from the magnetic bearing (45°), which equals 33°. Dial this revised bearing into your compass.

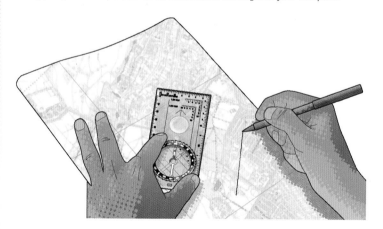

TRANSFERRING THE BEARING ONTO THE MAP
Place the top left corner of the compass base plate over the feature
on your map. Then, rotate the entire compass until the orienting
lines are parallel with the vertical grid lines. Draw a line from the
feature along the left side of the base plate to map your bearing.

Finding your position

If you are unsure of your position but can see features on the ground that you also recognize on your map, you can take bearings on these features with a compass and transfer them onto your map (see opposite) to accurately determine where you are. This is called "triangulation" and, in military terminlogy, "resection."

AT A KNOWN FEATURE

If you are at or on a known feature on a map—such as a river, road, or track—and can see another recognizable feature, you can take a bearing on that feature and mark it on your map. Where that line crosses your known feature is your position. In the example below, you know you are along the banks of a river and can see a church that you can identify on your map.

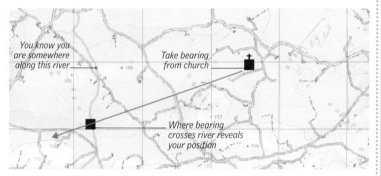

You know you are somewhere along this river

Take bearing from church

Where bearing crosses river reveals your position

NOT AT A KNOWN FEATURE

If you're not at a known feature, but can recognize features on the ground and locate them on your map, you can take bearings on them and transfer them to your map. To do this, you need two features at least $^6/_{10}$ mile (1km) away and at least 40° apart. After transferring both bearings, the point at which the two lines cross is your exact location.

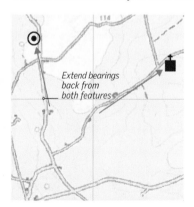

Extend bearings back from both features

Where two lines cross indicates your location

1 Using your compass, take bearings to the features on the ground.
• Transfer these bearings to back bearings (see box, p.44), and draw them on the map from your chosen features.

2 Extend these lines farther over the map until they cross each other.
• The point at which the lines cross shows your location.
• If you want to be more accurate, repeat the process with a third feature.

Calculating distance

There are several methods of calculating the distance you are walking, and a seasoned hiker will always use at least two of them at any one time.

PACE COUNTING

This involves knowing how many paces you take to cover a set distance and then counting them as you travel. There are many methods to do this. You can cut 10 notches in your walking stick and move a rubber band down a notch every 100m. Alternatively, place 10 pebbles in your pocket. For every 100m traveled, put a pebble in the other pocket. Most people take about 60 paces (120 steps) every 100m.

When rubber band reaches bottom notch, you have covered 1km

USING CUT-OFF FEATURES

Use your map to choose some key features on your route, and work out the distance between these. As you pass them, check them off mentally or mark your progress on the map. You'll then be able to keep track of the distance traveled when you reach each one of these spots.

NAISMITH'S RULE

Naismith's rule considers distance and topography, and is used to estimate the duration of hikes.
- Allow one hour for every 3 miles (5km) you will travel.
- Add 30 minutes for every 1,000ft (300m) you will climb.
- Subtract 10 minutes for every 1,000ft (300m) you will descend. However, for very steep slopes, add 10 minutes for every 1,000ft (300m) you will descend.

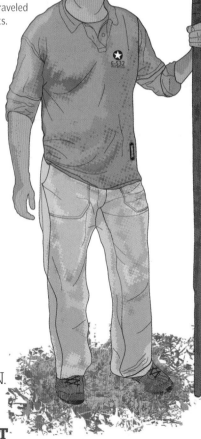

" BREAK YOUR ROUTE DOWN INTO SMALL SECTIONS FOR FOCUSED NAVIGATION. TRY TO **INCLUDE WATER SOURCES** AND A **SAFETY POINT** ON YOUR ROUTE. **"**

Navigation techniques

When navigating across land, you're less likely to get lost if you take direct bearings from one feature to another. However, at times, obstacles such as lakes may be directly in your path and you may consider walking around them rather than walking over or through them.

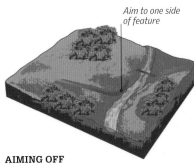

Aim to one side of feature

AIMING OFF

If you were aiming for a footbridge over a stream and didn't arrive exactly at the bridge, you would need to guess whether to turn left or right to reach it. By deliberately aiming off to one side (also called "deliberate off-set"), you can guarantee this direction.

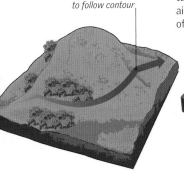

Curve your route to follow contour

CONTOURING

Climbing up and down hills can expend a lot of energy. The "contour navigation" technique involves walking at the same height around a feature, which will conserve energy.

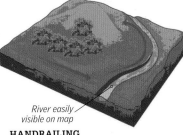

River easily visible on map

HANDRAILING

Following long linear features that run in the general direction of your travel, such as rivers or roads, can be a good way of navigating. Since these features are easy to follow, navigation becomes simpler.

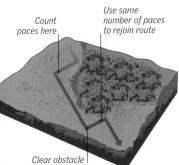

Count paces here

Use same number of paces to rejoin route

Clear obstacle

DETOURING (BOXING AN OBJECT)

If a straight-line bearing is impossible, use a compass to calculate four 90° turns to walk on to pass the obstacle. Count your paces on the first and third detours to return to your original route.

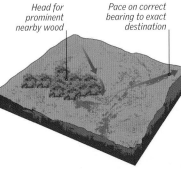

Head for prominent nearby wood

Pace on correct bearing to exact destination

STAND OFF/ATTACK POINT

This is useful when navigating to a specific point that may be difficult to locate. Aim initially for a nearby prominent feature, calculate a distance and bearing from it, and use pacing to locate the point.

Navigating without a compass

If you don't have a compass, you can use items from your survival kit to determine direction. It's fairly easy to improvise a compass using a piece of magnetized ferrous metal, but its accuracy depends on the materials available to you and your own ingenuity.

> **TOOLS AND MATERIALS**
>
> Improvised needle or razor blade, plus one of following:
> - Knife
> - Magnet
> - Battery and wire; paper and tape

Sourcing and magnetizing the needle

If your compass is damaged, you could still use its needle, which will already be magnetized. If this is unusable, you'll need a piece of ferrous metal to magnetize. This could be a needle, a razor blade, a paperclip that has been opened up and straightened out, or a small nail or straightened staple. The smaller and thinner your improvised needle, the easier it will be to magnetize. Use one of the following methods:

USING A MAGNET
Stroke the magnet along the needle's length repeatedly in one direction. The end of the magnetized needle that attracts to the south pole of the magnet will point north. Carry a magnet with you at all times, but never keep it near your compass, since it will affect its accuracy.

Repeated stroking increases effectiveness of magnetization

Allowing the needle to float freely

Once the needle is magnetized, it must turn freely to indicate direction. Protect it from elements, such as the wind, that will affect its movement.

SUSPENSION METHOD
The advantage of this method is that the equipment is portable and reusable. It works best with a magnetized razor blade, which will balance well. Attach the blade to a cotton thread and suspend it inside a plastic bottle. If the bottle's neck is too narrow to fit the blade through, remove the base of the bottle instead.

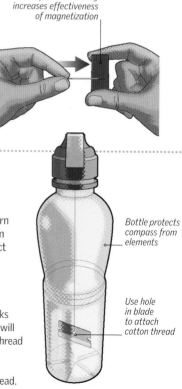

Bottle protects compass from elements

Use hole in blade to attach cotton thread

USING ELECTRICITY

The most effective way to magnetize a needle is to pass a small electrical current around it. Use a battery and insulated wire; alternatively, use brass snare wire and insulate it using something non-conductive, like paper.

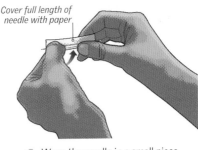

Cover full length of needle with paper

1 Wrap the needle in a small piece of paper, which will insulate it from the electrical current.

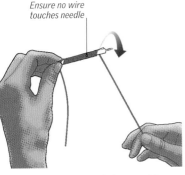

Ensure no wire touches needle

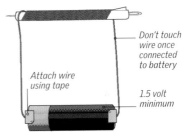

Don't touch wire once connected to battery

Attach wire using tape

1.5 volt minimum

2 Wrap the wire tightly around the full length of the insulated needle.

3 Attach the wire to the battery until the battery starts to get warm—this indicates that the process is complete.

PRINCIPLES OF MAGNETIZING

Usually, the longer you work on the needle, the stronger and more long-lasting the magnetization will be. To tell when it is magnetized enough, hold it up against another metal object. If it is attracted to the metal and can hold itself against it, it is strong enough. Then, allow it to float freely (see below), and determine which end points north by using natural aids like the Sun (see pp.52–54). Mark the north end with a pen or a small scratch.

FLOATING METHOD

In a sheltered place, float the needle on the surface of some water—for example, a puddle or a small, non-magnetic container filled with water. Balance the needle on a small, dry leaf (or piece of paper, piece of bark, blade of grass, or inside a shortened straw). The needle will rotate, settle, and align itself.

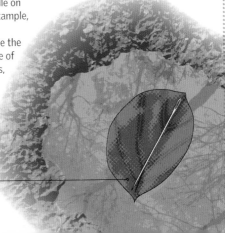

Leaf enables needle to float on water's surface

Using the Sun to navigate

When visible, the Sun is the clearest natural signpost to the four cardinal points (north, south, east, and west). It rises in the east and sets in the west, approximately. At noon, it is due south in the northern hemisphere and due north in the southern hemisphere. Use the Sun's course across the sky to determine direction and approximate the time.

Orientation

Tracking the movement of the Sun across the sky using a shadow stick will provide an indication of its direction of travel. The Sun moves from east to west at 15° an hour.

SHADOW STICK BASICS

Use a shadow stick to determine time and direction between the Arctic (66.5°N) and Antarctic Circles (66.5°S). The shadow will be north of the east-west line in the northern hemisphere, and south of the line in the southern hemisphere. When the shadow is at its shortest, it is noon.

1 Drive a stick into a piece of level ground, as upright as possible.

2 Place a stone at the tip of the stick's shadow.

3 Wait three hours and place a second stone at the new position of the shadow's tip.

4 Draw a line between the stones to find east-west; the first stone will be at due west and the second at due east.

5 To find north-south, mark a line at 90° to the east-west line.

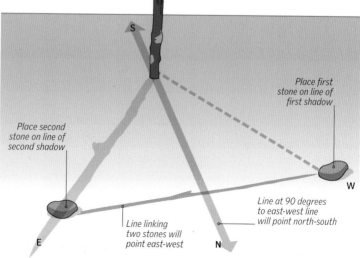

Stick should be approximately 3ft (1m) high

Place first stone on line of first shadow

Place second stone on line of second shadow

Line at 90 degrees to east-west line will point north-south

Line linking two stones will point east-west

S

W

E

N

Using the Sun to tell the time

Once you have established the east-west and north-south lines (see opposite), you can turn the shadow-stick apparatus into a sundial, to get an approximate idea of the time using the Sun's course across the sky.

1 Place the stick at the intersection of the north-south and east-west lines.

2 Tie a piece of cord to the stick. Attach a smaller stick to the other end of the cord and use it to draw a 180-degree arc between the two marker stones.

3 Divide the arc into 12 equal sections and mark each division with a notch. The notches represent one hour of time, from 6am to 6pm.

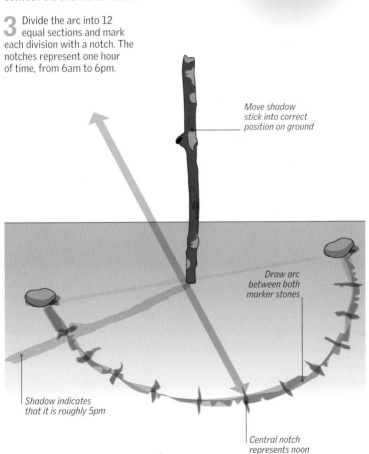

Move shadow stick into correct position on ground

Draw arc between both marker stones

Shadow indicates that it is roughly 5pm

Central notch represents noon

Using an analog watch to navigate

If you can see the Sun, you can use an analog watch as a protractor to determine an approximate direction. Ensure it is set to the correct local time and that you have taken daylight savings (DST) into account. If you don't have a watch but know the time, draw a watch face on a piece of paper, marking 12 o'clock and the hour hand. This method is increasingly less effective as you near the equator.

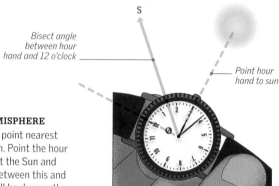

Bisect angle between hour hand and 12 o'clock

Point hour hand to sun

NORTHERN HEMISPHERE
Here, the cardinal point nearest to the Sun is south. Point the hour hand of a watch at the Sun and bisect the angle between this and 12 o'clock. This will be due south.

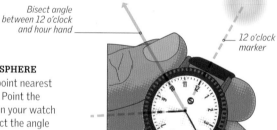

Bisect angle between 12 o'clock and hour hand

12 o'clock marker

SOUTHERN HEMISPHERE
Here, the cardinal point nearest to the Sun is north. Point the 12 o'clock marker on your watch at the Sun and bisect the angle between 12 o'clock and the hour hand. This will be due north.

NATURAL SIGNPOSTS
You can study the natural environment for orientation tips. This is useful if you know the predominant wind direction of an area.

TREES AND PLANTS
• Windswept trees point away from the wind; tree growth is fullest on sides facing the Sun.
• Moss and lichen grow in the shade.
• Some plants, such as the barrel cacti, twist toward the Sun as they grow.

ANIMALS AND INSECTS
• In very windy areas, small animals and birds tend to nest or burrow on the lee-side of hills.
• Spiders spin webs out of the wind.

SNOW AND ICE
• In powder-snow conditions, snow "dunes" often form parallel to the prevailing wind.
• Frost erosion is most severe on slopes facing the Sun.

Using the stars to navigate

You can orientate yourself by spotting certain stars. In the northern hemisphere, Polaris, located above due north on the horizon, can be found by locating the Big Dipper. In the southern hemisphere, you can work out the position of south on the horizon by finding the Southern Cross.

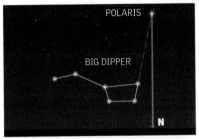

NORTHERN HEMISPHERE

Find the Big Dipper and project a line from the top of its two front stars. Follow this line until you find Polaris, located about four times the distance from the Big Dipper as the distance between its two front stars.

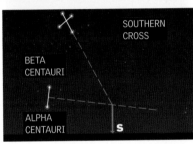

SOUTHERN HEMISPHERE

Project a line from the longer axis of the Southern Cross until you find a dark area of sky. Project a second line at 90° from the midpoint between two bright stars in the Centaurus constellation. Due south is below the point where these lines meet.

Using the Moon to navigate

Reflecting the light of the Sun, the Moon rises in the east and sets in the west, so it can be used for orientation. A shadow stick will work on a cloudless, full-Moon night.

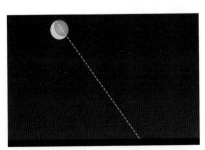

CRESCENT MOON

A line vectored between two horns of a crescent Moon will lead to a point that is approximately south on the horizon in the northern hemisphere, and roughly north in the southern hemisphere.

Traveling on foot

Hiking is a great way to explore wilderness terrain. It's important to have a decent level of fitness before you set out, and to wear and carry appropriate clothing and equipment. Hiking requires basic skills—using the correct techniques will help you move more efficiently, and ensure that your trip is safe.

Basic walking skills

Aim for a slow, even pace that can be maintained for the duration of the hike by all members of the group. A good way to do this is to develop a hiking rhythm. Take regular rest breaks and, if you're walking in a group, ensure that everyone knows the route.

Uphill techniques

When traveling uphill, lean forward slightly, and maintaining your momentum, shorten your stride. Keep your feet flat on the ground when pushing upward, and move your legs forward from the hips.

Backpack must fit properly for comfort

Carry walking stick for support while ascending

Deep tread grips ground and reduces slipping

Swing your arms for momentum and balance

Break in new boots before long hikes to avoid blisters

Downhill techniques

Walking downhill can place a lot of strain on your thighs, knees, and ankles, especially when you're carrying a heavy backpack. Be careful not to lose control or gather too much speed. Use your arms for balance and maintain a steady rhythm.

Lean backwards slightly

WALKING AT NIGHT

Unless you're in the desert and it's cooler to move in darkness, avoid walking at night because of nocturnal predators and navigational difficulties. If there's no alternative, try the following:
- Use your flashlight or improvise a torch by setting alight some birch bark or something similar.
- If this isn't possible and you've got the time, close your eyes for 20 minutes so they adjust to night vision.
- Use your walking stick to feel for obstacles, tripping hazards, or sudden drops.
- Keep your pace slow and deliberate, and check your compass regularly.

Negotiating difficult ground

One of the most challenging terrains to hike over is "scree," a mass of small rocks that slides underfoot, making uphill and downhill travel difficult. The slippery surface can make progress slow. Using correct techniques will help you to advance confidently, efficiently, and safely on scree.

TRAVERSING SCREE

Choose a zigzag route and look for a path that contains similar-sized rocks. Walk sideways across the slope, taking small steps and testing rocks for stability before placing your full weight on them.

Rocks at edge of slope are likely to be larger and more stable

Crossing rivers

River crossings are dangerous and should be avoided unless absolutely necessary. In a survival situation, once you are cold and wet—which can lead to hypothermia—it is hard to get warm and dry. Always check your map for routes around the river, and choose the safest available crossing point.

Crossing safely

Before you get into the water, make sure you have a change of clothes or means of getting dry on the other side. In cold conditions, collect everything you need to get a fire going (tinder, kindling, and dry wood), and keep this dry as you cross.

WADING BASICS

Wear footwear when wading, to protect your feet from rocks and other dangers. Remove pants to keep them dry and decrease resistance in the water. Use a walking stick for added support.

Choosing your crossing point

Walking upstream generally leads to shallower water, but be aware that even shallow water can have strong currents, as can water that looks calm on the surface. Always check for bridges farther up or downstream.

Exposed rocks can be slippery

Unusual variations in water flow could indicate submerged rocks

Don't cross on outside of bends where water flows faster

Lean on pole as you move your feet

Trees on opposite bank provide shelter from wind after you exit water

Shallow banks make entering and exiting water easier

Gravel shoal could make good halfway point, but be aware of fast-flowing water channeled around it

DIRECTION OF CURRENT

Cross downstream of debris or fallen trees

Wading with others

Crossing in a group is safer than crossing alone. Linking your arms together creates a stronger, more stable structure against the current, and provides backup for anyone who falls. Loosen the straps of your backpack, and place only one arm through them, so you can release the pack quickly if you fall.

Lean slightly into center

Place arms on each other's shoulders

DIRECTION OF TRAVEL

DIRECTION OF CURRENT

Strongest person bears main force of water

CROSSING IN A HUDDLE

Positioning the strongest person upstream, with the others providing stability and support, link your arms tightly and take short, deliberate steps across the river.

Loosen straps of backpack

Lightest person crosses in middle

Person bearing main force of current takes lead

DIRECTION OF TRAVEL

DIRECTION OF CURRENT

CROSSING IN A LINE

Keeping well-balanced, cross the river perpendicular to the current. Move slowly and position each step carefully to avoid being swept away by the force of the water.

> **USE YOUR WALKING STICK TO ASSESS CHANGES IN THE DEPTH OF THE RIVERBED.**

Extreme survival: in the mountains

WHAT TO DO

ARE YOU IN DANGER?

If you are in a group, try to help any others who are in danger

◄ NO   YES ►

Get yourself out of it:
Elements—Find or improvise shelter immediately
Animals—Avoid confrontation
Injury—Stabilize condition and apply first aid

► **ASSESS YOUR SITUATION** ◄
See pp.154–57

▼

DOES ANYONE KNOW YOU ARE MISSING OR WHERE YOU ARE?

If no one knows you are missing or where you are, you must notify people of your plight by any means

◄ NO   YES ►

If you are missed, a rescue party will almost certainly be despatched to find you

▼

DO YOU HAVE ANY MEANS OF COMMUNICATION?

You are faced with surviving for an indefinite period—until you are located or you find help

◄ NO   YES ►

If you have a cell or satellite phone, let someone know your predicament. If your situation calls for emergency rescue, and you have a Personal Locator Beacon (PLB), consider this option

▼

CAN YOU SURVIVE WHERE YOU ARE? *

If you cannot survive where you are and there are no physical reasons why you should remain, move to a location that offers a better chance of survival, rescue, or both

◄ NO   YES ►

Address the Principles of Survival: Protection; Location; Water; Food

▼   ▼

YOU WILL HAVE TO MOVE *

YOU SHOULD STAY *

YOU WILL HAVE TO MOVE **	YOU SHOULD STAY **

DO

- Keep all clothing dry and clean
- Collect drinking water from fast-moving streams; purify if you have the means
- Watch out for signs of cold-related injuries such as frost nip, frostbite, and hypothermia
- Regulate your clothing to avoid overheating when moving and hypothermia when static
- Use a walking stick to aid safe movement
- Watch the weather closely and be prepared to change your plans quickly—mountain climates are highly unpredictable
- Improvise shelter

DO

- Select a shelter site that offers protection from the elements
- Fill plastic bags or spare clothing with dry foliage and use as a mattress or pillow for insulation from the cold, damp ground
- Deploy all your aids to location and prepare for immediate use
- Check upstream for the quality of your water source
- Light a fire and (if in a group) take turns tending it to keep it going all night
- Continually reassess your situation and adapt your actions accordingly
- Be alert for signs of rescue

DON'T

- Descend hills carelessly; zigzagging across hills puts less strain on leg muscles
- Travel at a fast pace—high altitude equals less air and will place greater demands on even a fit person
- Sweat too much, because the moisture will chill you even further
- Ignore opportunities to collect dry tinder/kindling and fuel

DON'T

- Allow your extremities to get too cold as those areas are most susceptible to frostbite
- Overlook the dangers of carbon monoxide poisoning in cramped shelter. Don't let candles, cookers, or fires burn all night
- Breathe on your hands to warm them: you are exhaling warm air that you'll have to replace with cold

* If you cannot survive where you are, but you also cannot move because of injury or other factors, you must do everything you can to attract rescue.

** If your situation changes (for instance, you are "moving" to find help, and you find a suitable location in which you can stay and survive) consult the alternative "Dos" and "Don'ts."

Moving over snow

When hiking over frozen terrain, you must be physically fit—the conditions make for slow, exhausting progress. You should also have the right equipment and know how to use it. Wearing snow shoes or skis, and breathable, layered clothing, is essential.

Using snow shoes and skis

Snow shoes and skis are an effective way of traveling over snow. They work by spreading your body weight over a larger surface area, which enables you to walk on the surface of the snow rather than sink into it. Always set off cold, since you'll warm up quickly, and add or remove layers as required.

WARNING

Walking over snow without snow shoes is dangerous—sinking into the snow will leave you exhausted and wet, which, in cold conditions, can quickly lead to hypothermia, particularly when you stop and are no longer generating heat.

Ski mask protects eyes from glare

Wear backpack to keep both arms free

Shoe's ability to pivot reduces drag and improves maneuverability

Waterproof pants or gaiters keep legs dry

Snow shoes stop you from sinking into snow

Ski poles can be used to test snow ahead

Making improvised snow shoes

If you don't have pre-manufactured snow shoes, you can make simple shoes to help you negotiate the snow more effectively, using a knife, green wood, and cordage.

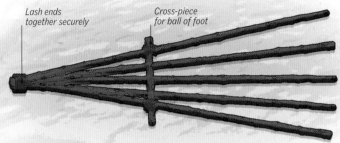

Lash ends together securely

Cross-piece for ball of foot

1 Cut five lengths of green wood. They should be as thick as your thumb and as long as the distance from your foot to your armpit. Cut three shorter lengths for cross-pieces.
• Lash the ends of the longer pieces together securely with cordage.
• Calculate where the ball of your foot will be positioned on the shoe and lash a cross-piece across the five lengths. Ensure that the shoe will balance.

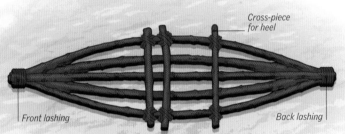

Cross-piece for heel

Front lashing

Back lashing

2 Securely lash the five loose lengths of wood together at the back of the shoe.
• Fix the second cross-piece roughly 2in (5cm) behind the first.
• Lash the third cross-piece where your heel will rest.
• Repeat steps 1 and 2 to make a second shoe before progressing to step 3.

Heel should lift off shoe slightly

3 Place your foot on top of the snow shoe, ensuring that the ball of your foot sits directly over the front cross-piece and that your heel is positioned on the back cross-piece.
• Tie your boot to the snow shoe using whatever cordage you have, but ensure that the heel remains free to pivot.

Alternative methods

There are many other methods of spreading your weight to help you move over snow. If you have no gaiters, tie plastic bags around the bottom of your legs to keep them dry.

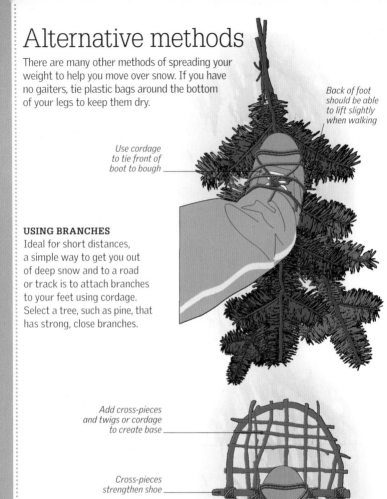

Back of foot should be able to lift slightly when walking

Use cordage to tie front of boot to bough

USING BRANCHES
Ideal for short distances, a simple way to get you out of deep snow and to a road or track is to attach branches to your feet using cordage. Select a tree, such as pine, that has strong, close branches.

Add cross-pieces and twigs or cordage to create base

Cross-pieces strengthen shoe

USING SAPLINGS
You will need branches that have some flexibility. Gently bend the longest branch into a teardrop shape and lash the two ends together. Heating the saplings over a fire will make them easier to bend.

ff ATTACHING BRANCHES TO YOUR FEET **USING CORDAGE** WILL ALLOW YOU TO GET **OUT OF DEEP SNOW**. **"**

Human power

Pulling your equipment behind you using a pulk is an extremely efficient way of moving over snow. Pulks are small, low-slung toboggans, typically made from lightweight plastic, and they come in different sizes.

TRAVELING WITH A PULK

Although pulks are the most efficient method of carrying heavy loads over snow using human power, they can be hard work, especially in softer snow. Wear breathable clothing to prevent overheating. Know how to release your harness quickly in an emergency. If you are in a group, one person can be harnessed to the rear of the pulk to act as a brakeman when going downhill.

Use harness to attach pulk to body

Pulk can be used to carry equipment or person

THE PULK PICKS UP SPEED EASILY, SO TAKE CARE WHEN TRAVELING DOWN SLOPES.

SNOW AND ICE
Knowing how to deal with different types of snow and ice is invaluable when you are hiking over frozen terrain.

DEEP SNOW
• If in a group, walk in single file and take turns in front—the most strenuous position, since you're creating the path.
• Avoid rocks—in spring, they absorb heat and the snow above becomes unstable.

FROZEN CRUST
• Test the snow ahead with a walking stick.
• If you come across melted depressions, called "sun cups," cross on the rims to keep from sinking into the snow.

SLOPES
• Kick firmly into the slope and test your weight before ascending. When descending, you can ski without your skis ("boot skiing").

ICE
• Use a walking stick to test the ice, especially over rivers and lakes. If in a group, rope yourselves together.
• Wear crampons for extra grip.
• Use an ice ax to cut steps on steep slopes, and to halt a fall.

GLACIERS
• Never cross glaciers without a guide, since glaciers require specialized skills.

Off-road driving

Four-wheel-drive (4WD) vehicles enable you to switch manually between two-wheel-drive, for roads, and four-wheel-drive, for low-traction conditions. The difference is the number of wheels powered at a time. Take care not to hook your thumbs around the steering wheel when driving over rough terrain. Hitting a rut can jerk the wheel and break it.

CHOOSING A ROUTE
When unsure about the conditions immediately ahead, walk the route first, checking for potential problems and options for self-recovery and escape. Where necessary, mark the route you have walked and follow these markers when you drive.

WHEN TO ENGAGE 4WD
Using 4WD takes a lot of fuel and should be avoided on hard roads due to the risk of damaging tires and gears. Use this option on rough terrain. It allows you to travel in low gear and gives a far superior traction.

Driving over difficult terrain

In a 4WD, all four wheels can be powered by the engine together (gasoline engines are usually more powerful, but diesel ones last longer and work well at low speeds). The principle behind 4WD is to reduce your chances of getting stuck—not to let you go farther until you do get stuck.

DRIVING AS A TEAM
Driving off-road over rough terrain is both mentally and physically tiring. Take regular breaks and share the driving if in a group. Always have at least two people in your vehicle—a driver and a spotter (responsible for navigation).

MAXIMUM TRACTION
On soft surfaces, lowering your tire pressure can improve traction. Place a brick $1/2$in (1cm) from the side of a rear tire on flat ground, deflate the tire until it touches the brick, measure this pressure, and apply to all four tires. Make sure you can reinflate them.

DRIVING ON SAND
In soft sand, tires tend to move the sand from the front of the tire to its rear. If movement is halted at all, the wheel can dig itself into a hole. To avoid this, continually steer from side to side, so the tire steers out of its own ruts. Avoid rapid changes in speed.

Apply plenty of engine power

Lower your tire pressure slightly

MUDDY TRACKS

Driving in mud requires concentration and the ability to adapt to different conditions. In deep mud, use wide tires or lower the tire pressure; but a hard surface below the mud will make things worse. Steering outside existing track ruts will probably give the best traction.

Deep tread helps vehicle to grip track

DRIVING ON SNOW AND ICE

This requires very smooth driving methods. Apply gradual pressure to the accelerator and brakes to avoid wheel spin. Use low gears, especially when going downhill. Practice fitting snow chains before you need them.

Snow chains give additional traction

CROSSING WATER

Always walk your route before driving across water. If the water seems too deep or the current too fast, do not cross. Always drive at the correct speed—too fast will send water everywhere, but driving too slowly may flood the engine bay.

Water level should not rise above top of wheels

Fit drain holes if applicable

Recovery from soft ground

Although using the correct techniques will help you cross soft ground, it's important to know what to do if you get stuck. Ideally, you should set out on a driving expedition with at least two vehicles. A second vehicle can be used for winching, dealing with breakdowns, or driving for help.

Basic recovery techniques

If you get stuck, don't try to aggressively free your vehicle—you might dig yourself into a deeper rut. Calmly evaluate your options (reversing or pushing, digging, using branches, and winching), and proceed.

Be cautious of vehicle rolling back

REVERSING OR PUSHING

If you can't free the vehicle using four-wheel drive, try alternating between reversing and driving forward in first gear.
- If this has no effect, ask the passengers to get out and push while you drive forward.

Try not to make holes deeper

Dig exhaust and chassis free if stuck

DIGGING

If reversing and pushing don't work, dig down in front of the wheels to create a slope that you can then drive up gently.
- Dig out the sand in front of each tire to create an upward slope.
- Avoid revving the engine.

Dig slope in front of all four wheels

USING BRANCHES

If the vehicle still won't move, place branches, wooden planks, sand ladders, or blankets—anything that will increase your traction— in front of the wheels. This gives the tires something to grip.
- Without revving the engine too much, gently ease the vehicle forward onto the branches or other material at a slow, steady speed.

Place branches in front of wheels

Winching

Use a cable attached to an electric-powered winching mechanism to pull the vehicle out of the hole via a strong anchor point. You can winch to another vehicle if you're traveling in convoy, although you risk both vehicles getting stuck. Use a natural anchor point if possible.

WARNING

When winching, don't stand within range of the cable in case it snaps under the strain. A breaking cable can cut a tree, or a person, in half. Place a blanket or sleeping bag over it.

NATURAL ANCHOR POINTS

Trees, large rocks, roots, or deadfalls can be used as anchor points. If using a tree, place the strap or cable near the ground, and use a winch strap to keep from damaging the tree. If the tree can't provide enough support, tie it to others in the vicinity.

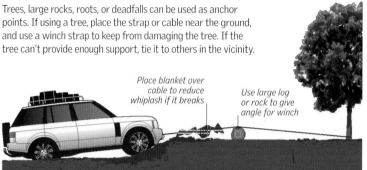

Place blanket over cable to reduce whiplash if it breaks

Use large log or rock to give angle for winch

BURIED ANCHOR POINTS

You can improvise an anchor by burying objects such as logs or a spare wheel. Dig a hole in the ground at least 3ft (1m) deep, attach your winch cable to your anchor, then bury the anchor in the hole. Refill the hole to secure it further. If using a tire, use the lever behind the spare wheel as an attachment point for the cable.

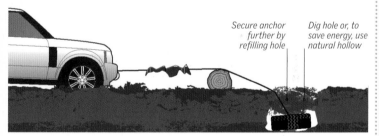

Secure anchor further by refilling hole

Dig hole or, to save energy, use natural hollow

WINCHING TO A STAKE

Stakes pushed into the ground can also provide an anchor point. You'll need a long, sturdy main stake—to which the winch cable is attached—and several supporting stakes, lashed together for added strength. Push the stakes into the ground at a slight angle.

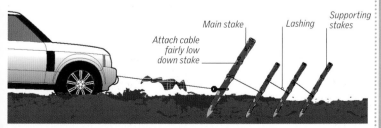

Main stake

Lashing

Supporting stakes

Attach cable fairly low down stake

Making a poncho float

It is useful to know how to build an improvised flotation aid or raft (see opposite), as you may find that a major water obstacle lies between you and rescue. A poncho float will keep your belongings dry and provide limited flotation as you cross the river. If you don't have a poncho, use any large piece of waterproof material.

Lay sheet on flat ground

1 Push your poncho hood to the inner side, and tightly secure its neck with drawstrings or cordage.
• Lay the poncho on the ground with the inner side facing upward.
• Place your kit on top.

Fold corners to prevent water from entering

2 Bring one side of the poncho up and over the equipment that is piled together in the middle.
• Repeat with the other three sides to create a rectangular package.

3 Wrap the float carefully to make it watertight. If you have a second poncho, repeat step 1, placing the float face down on the second sheet. Place brushwood in the float for added buoyancy.

4 Tie ropes, bootlaces, vines, or improvised cordage tightly around the float to secure it.
• As you enter the water, gently lower the float in with you. Pull it along as you cross the river.

Building rafts

Use any available materials to make a raft. Logs, bamboo, and discarded oil drums are naturally buoyant materials, and therefore, more effective. Most improvised rafts will float half-submerged, so build an extra raised platform.

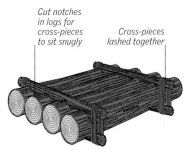

Cut notches in logs for cross-pieces to sit snugly

Cross-pieces lashed together

Openings must sit above water level

Tie drums to wooden platform

LOG RAFT
Use dry wood (standing deadwood is ideal) since this will float higher. The logs should be of the same diameter.

DRUM RAFT
Oil drums make ideal rafts. Always take care when handling chemical drums, as they may once have contained toxins.

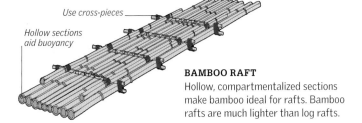

Use cross-pieces

Hollow sections aid buoyancy

BAMBOO RAFT
Hollow, compartmentalized sections make bamboo ideal for rafts. Bamboo rafts are much lighter than log rafts.

Making a paddle

In most cases, you can use the river current for momentum and your walking stick to maneuver the raft. However, if there is no current you will have to provide the propulsion yourself, and will need to improvise a paddle.

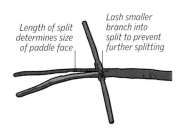

Length of split determines size of paddle face

Lash smaller branch into split to prevent further splitting

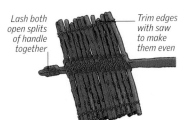

Lash both open splits of handle together

Trim edges with saw to make them even

1 Use a suitable length of green wood for the handle. This should be as wide as possible, but still comfortable to grip. Make a split in the end of the wood and insert smaller branches into it.

2 Continue to force smaller branches into the split, lashing each one until you have a sufficient paddle area. To make the paddle more rigid, lash the ends together.

Camp Craft

Camp Craft

Whether you intend to remain where you are and wait for rescue, move to a safer area and await rescue there, or walk out of the survival situation yourself, you're probably going to need to select a site on which to put up a shelter. This could be for just a single night or for a longer-term stay. A sound understanding of what constitutes a good location will allow you to address the basic principles of survival safely and effectively.

A well-organized site will not only give you a sense of purpose and order, but will also provide a safe environment for yourself and your equipment. Designating an area for storing equipment and tools, for example, will help prevent vital items from being lost and will reduce the likelihood of you or members of your team being injured.

A fire is an integral part of any campsite. It can be used for warmth, purifying water, cooking, signaling, for protection against wild animals, and for providing light when darkness falls. It also provides a sense of security. The psychological effects of being able to start a fire in a survival situation should never be underestimated; neither should the psychological effects of not being able to start one. Even in a survival situation, a simple camp can give a sense of normality and "home."

Learning skills that you can use in the wilderness is always a "work in progress." Knowing the correct method of using a knife, for example, will not only improve safety but will also mean that only the minimum amount of valuable energy is being used to complete a task. Equally, knowing how to tie a few simple knots will allow you to use whatever cordage you have in the most efficient way possible. The more knowledge you have of how something works, the more likely you are to be able to improvise what you need when you don't have it. This could mean the difference between continued survival and despair!

Using a space blanket

On any expedition, you should carry equipment—
such as a basic bivi or a tarpaulin—that could be
used to form a shelter should you need to protect
yourself from the elements.

A space blanket, however, is, quite simply, an
essential piece of gear—if you pack nothing else,
make sure you carry one and keep it with you at
all times. Space blankets pack down very small
and are available with one side silver (to reflect
heat) and one side bright orange (to aid location).
They can offer you immediate protection from the
elements in any environment, and can also be
converted into a basic shelter.

Producing a spark with a firesteel

A firesteel comprises two main parts: the material
that will produce the spark (usually a rod made
from ferrocerium or magnesium alloy) and a sharp
striker device (usually a knife blade or short piece
of hacksaw blade). When the striker is drawn over
the rod, a spark is produced.

To control the spark created by these two moving
parts, follow the method outlined below. It will
allow you to direct the spark accurately, reducing
your chances of scattering your tinder.

1 Place the rod in the center of the tinder. Position the
striker onto the rod and lock this hand in position.

2 Pull the rod up and away from the tinder, drawing
it against the striker.

3 To direct the sparks, alter the angle at which you
pull the rod up and away.

Organizing your site

Where you choose to set up your shelter depends on the environment, but always take into account the four principles of survival: protection, location, water, and food. Make sure there are no obvious dangers, and that you're able to signal for rescue.

WARNING

In any environment, it is possible that you will encounter potentially dangerous wild animals. Fortunately, most will avoid confronting you but they will defend themselves by attacking you if provoked, cornered, or surprised, particularly when they have young. If you see a bear, for example, stay calm, make yourself look as big as possible by raising your arms, and walk slowly backward (don't run). If the bear follows, hold your ground; if it attacks, play dead or fight back.

Latrine should be downwind of camp and downstream from water source

THREAT OF PREDATORS
If predators are around, hang unused food 10ft (3m) off the ground and 3ft (1m) away from the tree's trunk or branches.

Camp administration

It's important to organize your site, and establish disciplines and routines to ensure camp safety and reduce the risk of accidents. Designate specific areas—for storing equipment and firewood, and for cooking, and sleeping—and specific routines for activities (see panel, bottom).

ASSESSING YOUR ENVIRONMENT
It is vital to assess your campsite for potential dangers, such as animals, unstable rocks or trees, and flooding.

ANIMALS
Look for signs of animals, especially near water. Try to pitch your camp against a rock face so it can only be approached from one direction. Keep a fire going all night. Keep things on hand with which you can make a noise to scare off prowling predators. Don't camp near standing water where insects, such as mosquitoes, swarm.

WIND AND FLASH FLOODS
Position the entrance to your shelter at an angle to the wind. Gullies run the risk of flash floods or avalanches; inside river

Pitch your camp
near source of wood

Dig small runoff trench around
shelter to reduce risk of flooding
in heavy rain and to divert
water away downhill

Locate nearby
water source;
check water
upstream for
contamination

Assign open area for
location aids, and as
landing site for rescue
helicopter (see pp.158–59)

SIGNAL FIRES
Build three signal
fires (see pp.160–61)
on open ground.

bends are prone to erosion and floods;
and a river might burst its banks on an
outside bend during a heavy downpour.

STANDING DEADWOOD
These are dead trees that have not yet
fallen, but could fall with heavy wind,
or the weight of rain or snow. This is
the best type of wood for kindling and
fire fuel (see pp.94–95).

DEADFALLS
These are dangerous branches that have
broken off a tree, but haven't yet fallen.
Trees like beech, ash, and yew drop their
branches without warning.

ROCKFALLS AND ICE FALLS
If camping near rocks, check for cracks.
Fires below them can cause rockfalls. In
the cold, ice sheets can suddenly fall.

Bedding for shelters

Cover the floor of your shelter with some form of bedding to keep your body from losing heat to the cold, hard ground through conduction. Use the driest materials available.

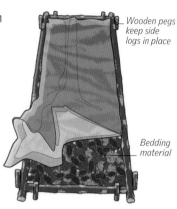

Wooden pegs keep side logs in place

Bedding material

BEDDING ESSENTIALS
- Collect twice as much bedding as you think you need, and surround it with logs to prevent it from spreading.
- Feathers, such as duck and goose down, are ideal—they retain heat but not moisture.
- Also try pine and spruce boughs, dry leaves, moss, bracken, and grasses.

Taking shelter in caves

Caves are ready-made shelters that are usually dry and secure. Possible dangers include animals, poor air quality, and water. Don't go farther in than you can see, as there may be hidden drops and slippery surfaces. Avoid old, disused mines as they may be prone to collapse.

ANIMAL DANGERS
Bears, bats, insects, spiders, and snakes all shelter in caves. Vampire bats are known to carry rabies; and bat droppings can be highly combustible.

POOR AIR QUALITY
If you feel light-headed or nauseated, or have an increased pulse and breathing rate, leave at once. If a flame dims or turns blue, it may be due to a lack of oxygen.

LIGHTING FIRES
If you build a fire at the front of a cave, smoke may blow back in and block your exit. Instead, build one to the rear of the cave, ensuring there is enough air flow.

THE DANGERS OF COASTAL CAVES
Beware of these signs of flooding during high tide: a line of seaweed, driftwood, or flotsam and jetsam; a damp smell; rock pools in or around the cave.

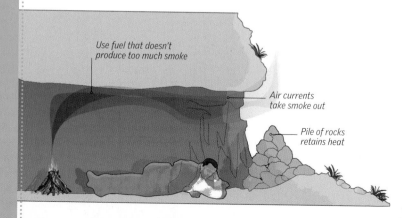

Use fuel that doesn't produce too much smoke

Air currents take smoke out

Pile of rocks retains heat

Corded A-frame

With a poncho, you can make a shelter for use in any environment and conditions. You can use a blanket, sheet, or tarpaulin in the same way. This poncho A-frame creates a tentlike shelter between two trees.

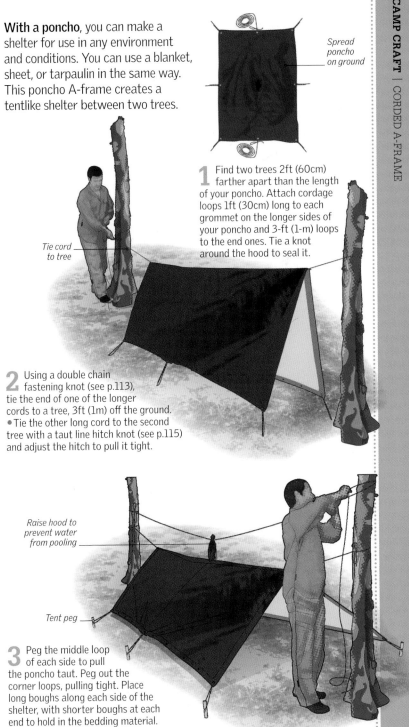

Spread poncho on ground

1 Find two trees 2ft (60cm) farther apart than the length of your poncho. Attach cordage loops 1ft (30cm) long to each grommet on the longer sides of your poncho and 3-ft (1-m) loops to the end ones. Tie a knot around the hood to seal it.

Tie cord to tree

2 Using a double chain fastening knot (see p.113), tie the end of one of the longer cords to a tree, 3ft (1m) off the ground.
• Tie the other long cord to the second tree with a taut line hitch knot (see p.115) and adjust the hitch to pull it tight.

Raise hood to prevent water from pooling

Tent peg

3 Peg the middle loop of each side to pull the poncho taut. Peg out the corner loops, pulling tight. Place long boughs along each side of the shelter, with shorter boughs at each end to hold in the bedding material.

Trench shelter

A natural hollow in the ground can be made into a trench shelter; even a shallow one can protect you from the wind if you lie in it. Avoid hollows in low-lying areas that may flood. If on a slope, avoid those exposed to runoff water. You can build trench shelters in varied types of terrain, including sand, snow, shoreline, and forests.

1 If the hollow is too shallow to lie in, remove some soil with a digging stick. Beware wet soil, since it could be prone to flooding.
- If the ground is too hard to dig, build up the sides with logs. Lay bedding material on the ground.

Sturdy digging stick with pointed end

Long log creates height and slope for pitched roof

2 With your saw, cut several sturdy poles or branches long enough to place across the hollow to create a supporting roof. Place a thicker, longer log on top of the cross poles for a pitched roof.

3 Place shorter branches, sticks, or poles on the log, and cross branches to create a pitched roof. Pack the material tightly together.
- Insulate the pitched roof with lots of foliage. Start the final layer at the ground and work up.

Space between support and pitched roof retains heat

Leave entrance at one end, 90° to wind

Forest A-frame

Although an A-frame can take several hours to build, it is simple to construct and easy to keep warm. A-frames can also be adapted into multiperson shelters.

TOOLS AND MATERIALS

- Knife
- Saw (or ax)
- Cordage
- Saplings
- Poles of various lengths
- Covering for walls—such as pine boughs, leaves, and moss

1 Smooth one side of a ridgepole with your knife, leaving one side bare and one with branch stubs.
● Hammer two poles into the ground to form an "A." Rest one end of the ridgepole on top of the "A" and the other on the ground.

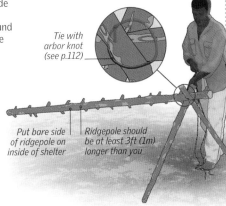

Tie with arbor knot (see p.112)

Put bare side of ridgepole on inside of shelter

Ridgepole should be at least 3ft (1m) longer than you

2 Lay poles against the stubs on the ridgepole, decreasing in height as you work from front (the "A") to back (the ground).
● At each junction, rest the side poles against the stubs or tie them to the ridgepole.

Cover framework from back to front and bottom to top

3 Weave alternating rows of saplings through the poles to make a framework for the covering, leaving an entrance near the front.
● Weave a thick layer of natural material—pine boughs, branches, and twigs—into a "thatch," and use it to cover the framework.

First layer prevents final layer from falling in

4 Cover the first layer with leaves, moss, and mulch, starting from the ground and working up to the ridgepole. Build a fire reflector at the entrance (see p.93).

Fire reflector

Forest lean-to

A lean-to has a sloping roof that leans against a horizontal ridgepole. It works best on a flat area between two trees or vertical supports secured firmly into the ground. If you're building a lean-to for a group, ask everyone to lie down next to each other and add an additional 6in (15cm) per person to establish how wide the shelter needs to be.

TOOLS AND MATERIALS
- Poles and stakes
- Saw and knife
- Cordage
- Saplings
- Foliage for roof covering

1 Place the ridgepole against the trees at the height you require, and lash it with an arbor knot (see p.112) to both trees.
- Place a support pole under the ridgepole and lash it to the trees. Peg a log where you want the foot of the shelter to be.

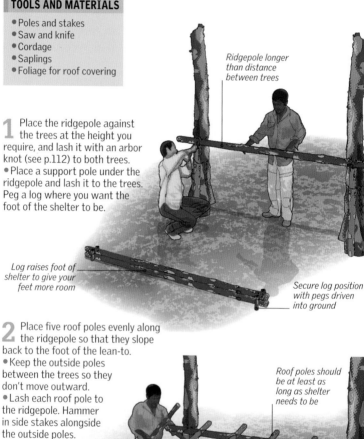

Ridgepole longer than distance between trees

Log raises foot of shelter to give your feet more room

Secure log position with pegs driven into ground

2 Place five roof poles evenly along the ridgepole so that they slope back to the foot of the lean-to.
- Keep the outside poles between the trees so they don't move outward.
- Lash each roof pole to the ridgepole. Hammer in side stakes alongside the outside poles.

Roof poles should be at least as long as shelter needs to be

Stakes along either side of shelter form walls

BUILDING IN A FOREST

Temperate forests provide many opportunities for shelter. Expend the least amount of energy for the most amount of protection—first, see what nature can provide before building a shelter yourself (see also pp.76–77).

POINTS TO REMEMBER

• Collect everything you need before you start building and before it gets dark.
• Make sure your aids to location can be seen or activated quickly (signal fires, heliograph, flares, radio signals).
• Think safety: if possible, wear gloves to clear leaves and debris from the ground for protection from spiders and snakes.
• Layer down your clothing as you work to prevent overheating.
• Make your shelter as waterproof as you can and ensure your bedding raises you at least 4in (10cm) off the ground.

3 Weave saplings in and out through the roof poles, working across and down from the ridgepole. Alternate the weave of each row, first horizontally, then diagonally. Weave smaller saplings through the side stakes to form walls.

Crisscross saplings over roof poles

Apply covering to roof and walls, laying large materials as base

To help rain runoff, lay covering from foot to ridgepole

4 With everyone in the same lean-to, you need to light only one fire.
• Layer the inside floor with dry material to form bedding.
• Establish a watch system to ensure the fire is maintained and controlled.

Bank final covering against walls to help insulation

Build fire reflector (see p.93)

Place pole between trees to keep bedding in place

Jungle A-frame

An A-frame is relatively easy to make. If you have a poncho, tarpaulin, shelter sheet, groundsheet, or another type of sheet, you'll need to modify it first to make it into a bed (see box, opposite).

TOOLS AND MATERIALS
- Long poles and ridgepole
- Cordage and pegs
- Knife, saw, machete, or parang
- Tarpaulin, groundsheet, poncho, or shelter sheet

Angle formed by "A" determines how far down legs of platform will sit

Wedge poles into ground

Tie junctions securely

1 Cut seven long poles that will take your weight. Tie two poles together with an arbor knot (see p.112) to form an "A." Tie the joint to a tree or tree branch.

2 Repeat step 1 to form an "A" for the other end, in line with the first "A." The distance between the two "A"s should be at least 2ft (60cm) longer than your height.

Tie poles of poncho to legs of A-frame

3 Put a ridgepole on top of the two "A"s, and tie it to both junctions for extra stability.

4 Position both poles of your poncho bed on the outside of the A-frame. Move them down until the sheet is taut.

BUILDING IN THE JUNGLE

Shelters in the rainforest need to be quick to erect, just big enough for your needs, and safe from animals (see also pp.76–77 and p.83).

CHECKLIST

• A cutting tool; ideally a parang, machete, or ax but a saw or bushcraft knife will suffice.
• Clear the ground around your shelter to deter animals. Use a makeshift brush, never your bare hands, so as not to be bitten by snakes or spiders.

• Build your shelter far enough off the ground to avoid being bothered by insects or any other animals—particularly those animals that move around at night.
• Avoid dehydration and heat-related injuries such as heat stress and heat stroke. Drink water frequently, take regular breaks in the shade, and don't work too fast.
• Inside your shelter, use a full mosquito net and a head-net.
• Build a fire in order to keep insects and animals away.

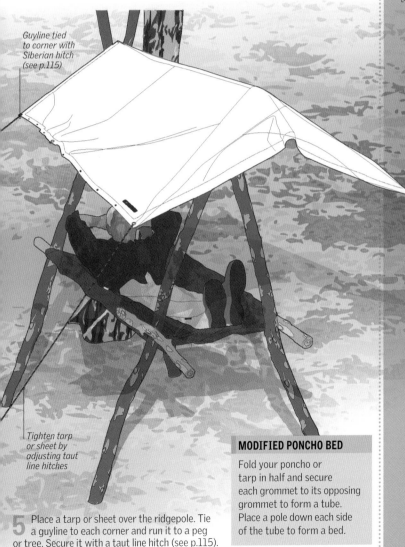

Guyline tied to corner with Siberian hitch (see p.115)

Tighten tarp or sheet by adjusting taut line hitches

5 Place a tarp or sheet over the ridgepole. Tie a guyline to each corner and run it to a peg or tree. Secure it with a taut line hitch (see p.115).

MODIFIED PONCHO BED

Fold your poncho or tarp in half and secure each grommet to its opposing grommet to form a tube. Place a pole down each side of the tube to form a bed.

Extreme survival: in the jungle

WHAT TO DO

ARE YOU IN DANGER?

If you are in a group, try to help any others who are in danger

◀ NO   YES ▶

Get yourself out of it:
Elements—Slow down your pace. Find or improvise immediate shelter
Animals—Avoid confrontation
Injury—Stabilize condition and apply first aid

▶ **ASSESS YOUR SITUATION** ◀
See pp.154–57

▼

DOES ANYONE KNOW YOU ARE MISSING OR WHERE YOU ARE?

If no one knows you are missing or where you are, you must notify people of your plight by any means

◀ NO   YES ▶

If you are missed, a rescue party will almost certainly be despatched to find you

▼

DO YOU HAVE ANY MEANS OF COMMUNICATION?

You're faced with surviving for an indefinite period—until you are located or you find help

◀ NO   YES ▶

If you have a cell or satellite phone, let someone know your predicament. If your situation is serious enough for emergency rescue, and you have a Personal Locator Beacon (PLB), consider this option

▼

CAN YOU SURVIVE WHERE YOU ARE? *

If you cannot survive where you are and there are no physical reasons why you should remain, move to a location that offers a better chance of survival, rescue, or both

◀ NO   YES ▶

Address the Principles of Survival: Protection; Location; Water; Food

▼   ▼

YOU WILL HAVE TO MOVE **   **YOU SHOULD STAY ****

YOU WILL HAVE TO MOVE **

YOU SHOULD STAY **

▼   ▼

DO

- Make an informed decision on the best location to move to

- Use line of sight to navigate on your bearing, since visibility may be less than 33ft (10m)

- Improvise a shelter when not moving, and sleep off the ground, clear of the damp floor and animals

- Look for dry tinder and fuel

- Follow water courses downstream. Transportation in the jungle relies on rivers, so settlements are most likely to be found alongside rivers

- Step onto logs to see what's on the other side, rather than stepping straight over onto an unseen snake

DON'T

- Use your hands to clear undergrowth—a machete or walking stick is better suited

- Drink untreated water

- Leave it too late in the day to stop and make camp— three hours before sunset is recommended

- Keep too quiet. Make a noise as you progress, to warn animals

DO

- Select a shelter site where you can sleep off the ground and where your location aids will be most effective

- Use a mosquito net or put damp foliage on your fire to repel insects, or cover exposed skin with mud

- Deploy all your aids to location and prepare them for immediate use. Be constantly alert for signs of rescue

- Keep yourself covered despite the heat—high humidity encourages infections. Also wash at every opportunity

- Keep a fire going to aid location and ward off insects

DON'T

- Let the oppressive nature of the jungle overwhelm you. Slow down to its pace

- Let your firewood get damp—store dry tinder and split or quarter wood to get to the dry inner core

- Eat what you cannot identify as edible—this could result in you becoming so sick that you cannot function

* If you cannot survive where you are, but you also cannot move because of injury or other factors, you must do everything you can to attract rescue.

** If your situation changes (for instance, you are "moving" to find help, and you find a suitable location in which you can stay and survive) consult the alternative "Dos" and "Don'ts."

Desert shelters

If you're planning a trip into the desert, take something you can use to improvise an immediate shelter from the Sun—for example, a shelter sheet or tarpaulin. You can either build a "scrape" in a natural hollow or erect a quick shelter above the ground using your poncho.

Desert scrape

If you have cord, you can dig a scrape and use the cord to peg out the sheet above it. Otherwise, the sheet will have to be held in place by soil, sand, or rocks. With all layered desert shelters, maintain tautness and separation between the layers.

Cordless scrape

You can make a cordless scrape by digging down or by building up the sides. Anchor your sheet with rocks.

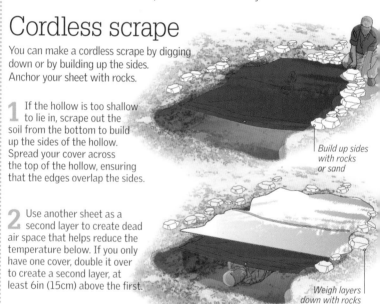

1 If the hollow is too shallow to lie in, scrape out the soil from the bottom to build up the sides of the hollow. Spread your cover across the top of the hollow, ensuring that the edges overlap the sides.

Build up sides with rocks or sand

2 Use another sheet as a second layer to create dead air space that helps reduce the temperature below. If you only have one cover, double it over to create a second layer, at least 6in (15cm) above the first.

Weigh layers down with rocks

BUILDING IN THE DESERT

This is a challenge because of the heat and potential lack of materials, so try to find a shaded site.

POINTS TO REMEMBER

- Avoid building your shelter during the hottest part of the day.
- Ration your sweat and not your water. If you start to sweat, take a break.
- Avoid low-lying areas, dry riverbeds, and wadis as there is a risk of flash floods.
- Avoid the tops of large hills due to the risk of lightning and extreme winds.

- Build your shelter on a small rise, where it can be much warmer at night.
- The opening should face north in the Northern Hemisphere and south in the Southern Hemisphere to avoid direct sunlight during the day.
- Dig down to create a depression, as the ground is cooler below the surface.
- Build your shelter for the worst possible conditions—desert weather is unpredictable.
- If your shelter sheet has a shiny side, make sure it faces up to reflect heat and act as a location aid.

Quick shelter

If you can't find a hollow, erect a poncho shelter (see p.79) in a place that keeps you cool during the day—for example, under trees or bushes, or at the top of a slight rise for a cool breeze.

1 Find a site beside a tree or secure a post next to where you want the shelter's opening to be.
• Rig a ridgeline to the tree or post, and peg your poncho over it to form a shelter.
• Repeat this with a second poncho, shelter sheet, or space blanket to create a separate layer.

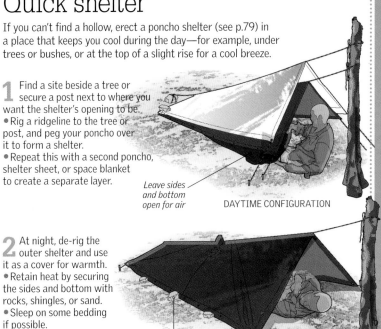

Leave sides and bottom open for air

DAYTIME CONFIGURATION

2 At night, de-rig the outer shelter and use it as a cover for warmth.
• Retain heat by securing the sides and bottom with rocks, shingles, or sand.
• Sleep on some bedding if possible.

Weigh down with rocks or sand to retain heat

NIGHTTIME CONFIGURATION

Para scrape

If you have cordage, tie your sheet to four posts. Otherwise, use your backpack or a pile of stones. Prepare the hollow as for a cordless scrape (see opposite). Tie the sheet to the posts, leaving a gap for air. Create a second layer above the first. Place foliage between the layers to maintain separation.

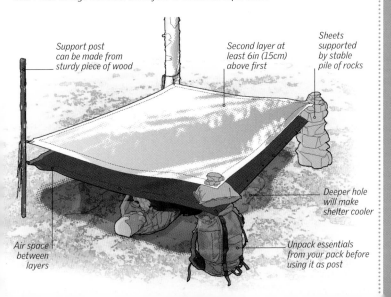

Support post can be made from sturdy piece of wood

Second layer at least 6in (15cm) above first

Sheets supported by stable pile of rocks

Deeper hole will make shelter cooler

Air space between layers

Unpack essentials from your pack before using it as post

Building a quinzhee

A quinzhee is a dome-shaped shelter made by hollowing out a pile of settled snow. It's an overnight shelter that is easier to construct than the more permanent igloo, which is made from cut blocks of snow and requires skill and knowledge. You can't stand up in a quinzhee, but you can sit upright or just curl up.

WARMING AND COOLING TIPS

The following tips may help you stay at the right temperature:
- Remove layers of clothing as you work, perhaps to your base layers, with a waterproof layer on top. Keep clothing dry so you can wear it when you stop working.
- Keep shelters at a constant temperature. If snow melts and refreezes, it stops insulating.
- Avoid heating your shelter too much.

1 Find a relatively flat area covered with snow. Mark out a circle for your shelter, including walls about 10in (25cm) thick, and stamp down the snow. Use your backpack and boughs or leaves, covered with a tarpaulin, to form the core of the shelter. Site the doorway at 90 degrees to the wind.

Cover backpack with tarpaulin

2 Use a mess can, pan, snow shoe, or other suitable item to gather as much soft snow as you can.
- Pile snow on the shelter's core to form a dome of the required height. Build up layers of snow until you have a covering of at least 10in (25cm), smoothing out each layer.
- Smooth out the snow on the dome and leave it to sinter (harden) for 1–3 hours.

CARBON MONOXIDE

Carbon monoxide is an odorless gas that's produced when there's not enough oxygen to create carbon dioxide from burning fuel. Carbon monoxide poisoning can be fatal in an environment that is well-insulated and non-ventilated.

PREVENTION IS BETTER THAN CURE

Create holes, 3–4in (7.5–10cm) in diameter, at the base and top of your shelter. Make sure the air flows out freely.

SIGNS OF POISONING

Carbon monoxide poisoning is cumulative and can build up over a few days. Mild effects of this are fatigue, faintness, and flulike symptoms. As the poisoning progresses, the effects are severe headaches, nausea, and decreased mental coordination.

TAKE ACTION

Get into fresh air at once. Breathe fresh air for at least four hours to reduce the carbon monoxide in your system by half.

3 To get an even thickness in the roof and walls, push guide-sticks of equal length through the snow toward the center of the dome.
• Build a small compact mound in front of the dome.

Mark each guide-stick at 12–18in (30–45cm) before inserting into snow

Scoop up snow into small mound for entrance

4 Burrow into the mound, remove your bag and tarp, and excavate snow from the core.
• Use the guide-sticks to keep the walls at least 10in (25cm) thick.
• Smooth out the snow on the inside to prevent drips from forming.
• Build a raised sleeping platform. This takes cold air away from your sleeping area.

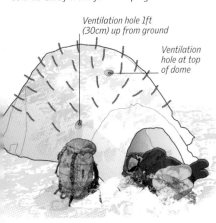

Ventilation hole 1ft (30cm) up from ground

Ventilation hole at top of dome

BUILDING SNOW SHELTERS

The following tips may help you to build a snow shelter:
• Snow is a good insulator. Fresh, uncompacted snow is typically 90–95 percent trapped air. Since the air barely moves, the snow can keep you warm and dry if used correctly.
• Check your site for hazards, such as snowdrifts, freezing winds, avalanches, cornice collapse, and big animals.
• Keep your tools inside the shelter in case you have to dig your way out.
• Brush snow off your equipment and clothing before entering the shelter.
• Tie all vital equipment to yourself so you don't lose it in deep snow.

Making fire

The ability to make and maintain a fire can be a significant psychological factor in deciding whether you do all you can to survive or just give up. Gather your materials first—a portable kit that keeps everything in one place is convenient.

Preparing beforehand

Starting a fire needs good prior preparation. Preparing the ground, your materials, and your equipment will usually make firelighting much easier and more likely to succeed.

CHOOSING YOUR GROUND

Be careful when selecting the place in which you intend to start a fire. Clear the ground in advance. Never light a fire directly on the ground and watch that the fire doesn't spread or burn out of control.

KEY POINTS TO REMEMBER

Always carry some form of firelighter. Practice your skills in different conditions, with different materials. Collect tinder as soon as you enter the forest. If it's wet, dry it in your pockets. Collect more than enough quantities of the materials needed to light a fire.

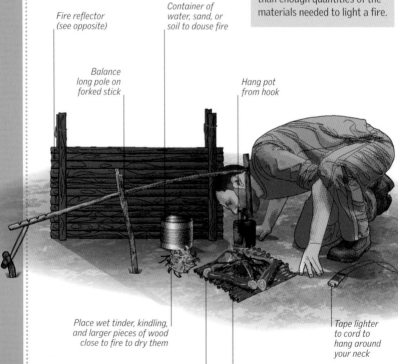

Fire reflector (see opposite)

Container of water, sand, or soil to douse fire

Balance long pole on forked stick

Hang pot from hook

Place wet tinder, kindling, and larger pieces of wood close to fire to dry them

Tape lighter to cord to hang around your neck

Green wood platform protects fire from ground moisture and limits heat dissipating into ground

Contain fire with green wood or dry, nonporous rocks that won't explode

Building a fire reflector

A fire reflector makes a fire more efficient as it directs the heat into your shelter. Construct your reflector so that you can build a fire about 3ft (1m) from the entrance to your shelter. An L-shaped end to the reflector will retain more heat.

Finish stack when it reaches required height

Stack poles to form wall

Use green wood so heat doesn't set reflector alight.

1 Check that the air flow will be across the reflector. Hammer two poles into the ground, a pole's width apart. Add a second set of poles.

2 Tie the tops of the upright poles together. Ensure the wall is as long as the shelter's entrance, to retain heat and keep out wind and rain.

Matchless fireset can

This contains a one-stop solution to getting a fire going in any weather condition. This small waterproof can, when taped, has all you need to make a fire: a sparking device, tinder, kindling, and fuel. Hexamine is scraped onto cotton, then a spark from the flint and steel ignites the cotton long enough for the fuel blocks to light.

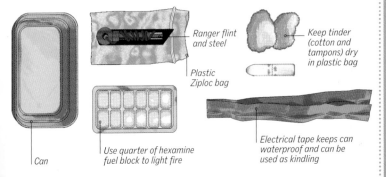

Ranger flint and steel

Keep tinder (cotton and tampons) dry in plastic bag

Plastic Ziploc bag

Use quarter of hexamine fuel block to light fire

Electrical tape keeps can waterproof and can be used as kindling

Can

COMPONENTS OF FIRE
Oxygen, heat, and fuel are crucial for a strong fire. The key is to achieve the best balance between them.

OXYGEN
If you smother the fire with too much wood, oxygen may not get to the flame. If the fire is dying, fan it with paper or your hand to create a draft that feeds oxygen to it.

HEAT
Heat is needed to ignite the fuel. It can be generated by a spark, a chemical reaction and friction, or by friction alone (see pp.100–01 and pp.104–07).

FUEL
Once the fire starts, you need fuel (see pp.94–95). Start with small, dry pieces that will generate enough heat to then burn increasingly large pieces.

The elements of fire

The three material elements you need to build
a fire are tinder, kindling, and fuel. They must be
dry and collected in sufficient quantities.

Tinder

The first element you use to make a fire is dry, combustible tinder. You
may have tinder in your equipment (see pp.96–97), or you may need to
find natural or other man-made sources. The key is to experiment with
what's around you before you actually need it. Make sure it's dry—leave
it in the sun if it's damp.

TYPES OF TINDER

Natural sources include feather sticks
(see opposite), bark and bamboo stem
shavings, plant and animal down, fine
wood dust, pine pitch, dead and dry
moss, and dry grass. Man-made sources
include cotton balls, lint, tampons,
tissue paper, camera film, rubber,
and candle wick.

EMERGENCY TINDER

Carry tinder, such as cotton balls
or a tampon, in a 35mm film
canister or a Ziploc bag. For each
fire, use some cotton or a small
piece of tampon. Cotton balls
smeared with petroleum jelly
make a flame last longer.

TINDER BUNDLE

To prepare the tinder to take a
spark or a coal, make it into a tinder
bundle (above). Vigorously tease, rub,
and pull the fibers with your fingers
until the bundle becomes a ball the size
of a grapefruit. Push the finest, most
combustible material into its interior
and mix up the tinder.

Kindling

Kindling is added to burning tinder
when it is dry. It can be as thin as
a match or as thick as a finger. If
it's damp, remove the outer bark
and break the kindling into sticks
6in (15cm) long.

TYPES OF KINDLING

Soft-wood twigs are very combustible,
while wood with flammable resin burns
hot and long. You can use some types of
tinder as kindling—such as bark, palm
leaves, pine needles, and grass—but you'll
need larger quantities than for tinder.

Fuel

Once the fire can sustain itself for
five minutes after initial tending, add
increasingly larger fuel to create a
good heart—a bed of hot coals that
sustains the fire. The fuel should be
as thick as your wrist or forearm.

TYPES OF FUEL

Hard woods from deciduous trees
(such as oak and maple) produce good
coals. Soft woods from conifers (such
as pine and fir) are easier to light, but
produce less heat. You can also use peat,
charcoal, and dried animal droppings.

Making a feather stick

A feather stick effectively provides tinder, kindling, and fuel on one piece of wood. Four to six feather sticks provide enough combustible material to get a fire going. Ideally, use standing dead wood. If using small, dead branches that have snapped off a tree, remove the bark first.

STANDING DEADWOOD

A tree that's died but hasn't fallen over has no green foliage, and the bark falls off without being replaced. This is the ultimate wood for firelighting, as it can provide kindling and fuel and, when split, makes excellent feather sticks. The bottom few inches may be wet where the tree wicks up moisture from the ground.

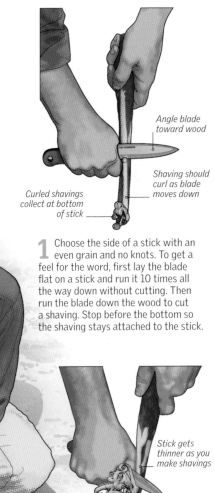

Angle blade toward wood

Shaving should curl as blade moves down

Curled shavings collect at bottom of stick

1 Choose the side of a stick with an even grain and no knots. To get a feel for the word, first lay the blade flat on a stick and run it 10 times all the way down without cutting. Then run the blade down the wood to cut a shaving. Stop before the bottom so the shaving stays attached to the stick.

Stick gets thinner as you make shavings

Keep stick firmly on ground to steady your action

Collect any shavings that fall from stick

2 Turn the stick slightly and run the knife down the edge created in step 1 to create a second shaving. Turn the stick again and repeat, working around it.

3 Continue to feather the rest of the stick. When you finish, you will have a thin stick with curled shavings still attached, and ready for use as kindling.

Making char cloth

An excellent form of tinder (see p.94), char cloth is cotton cloth that's been combusted in the absence of oxygen (pyrolysis). It is lightweight, takes up minimal space, and even from a weak spark, produces an ember extremely well. Char cloth works only when it is dry.

(see p.94)

TOOLS AND MATERIALS

- Can with tight-fitting lid, such as small shoe-polish can
- Nail
- 100 percent cotton cloth
- Knife or scissors
- Spark or flame

Punch hole into lid, if possible using nail

1 Turn the lid of a can upside-down and hammer a nail into the center. Usually, the smaller the hole, the better.

Put as many pieces of cloth of varied sizes as possible into can

Smooth out rough edges around hole

SUR-VVLOC

2 Cut cotton cloth into pieces that fit into the can without folding. Securely place the lid on the can.

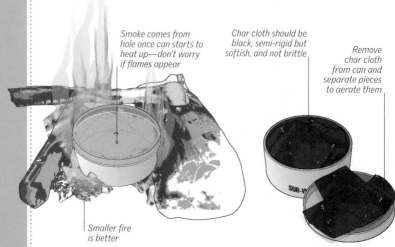

Smoke comes from hole once can starts to heat up—don't worry if flames appear

Smaller fire is better

3 Place the can on a fire to burn off all the oxygen inside the can. When the smoke stops, the process is complete.

Char cloth should be black, semi-rigid but softish, and not brittle

Remove char cloth from can and separate pieces to aerate them

SUR-V

4 Once the can cools down, examine the cloth. Strike a spark on a piece of cloth to check if it creates an ember.

Making a fire can

You can use a fire can to start a stubborn fire when conditions are less than perfect, or to boil water, do some basic cooking, or warm your hands. Once lit, a fire can burns for hours with a concentrated, controllable flame that produces no smoke.

TOOLS AND MATERIALS
- Can with tight-fitting lid, such as small shoe-polish can
- Cardboard (ribbed or plain)
- Candle and match or lighter
- Knife or scissors

Extra ¼in (4mm) of cardboard will burn down slightly and act as wick

Candle should be angled so flame melts wax rather than burning into air

1 Cut out a long, thin piece of cardboard ¼in (4mm) wider than the depth of your can. Roll it tightly along its length until the roll just fits inside the can.

2 Light your candle and let the melting wax drop into the can. Let it soak the cardboard and fill up the can. Stop when it nears the top and let it harden.

Can becomes hot so don't touch it

❝ WHEN THE FLAME STARTS TO FAIL, EITHER ADD TO THE WAX OR REPLACE THE CARDBOARD AND START AGAIN. ❞

3 When the can cools down, hold it at an angle and light the top of the cardboard with the candle. Let the flame spread across the top of the can.

Types of fire

Once you have collected your tinder, kindling, and fuel, and made sure it's dry and at hand, you can make your fire. You can choose different types of fire, depending on your needs (see opposite).

Choosing a fire

If you have a choice of fuel and can build a specific fire, see which one suits your needs (see opposite). Consider the function of the fire: warmth is probably your most urgent need, but other uses include cooking, signaling (see pp.160–61), drying wet clothing, and disposing of waste. Consider the availability of the required components. Estimate how much you'll need, and double it.

FIRE ESSENTIALS

These general tips will help in making fires:
• Choose a fire that requires the least effort for the maximum gain.
• It is more efficient to build a small fire and sit close to it, than to build a large fire and sit far away from it.
• If your wood is wet, remove the bark and split the wood—the center will usually be dry.
• Once the fire is established, place damp tinder, kindling, and larger pieces of wood close to the fire to dry out.

Light your fire

There are numerous ways to build a fire and get one going, and everyone has their favorite. The following example is a tried-and-true method that's versatile and works well in a variety of conditions.

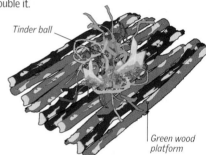

Tinder ball

Green wood platform

1 Place the tinder ball (see p.94) on a green wood platform. Light the tinder (see pp.100–01) and let it catch.

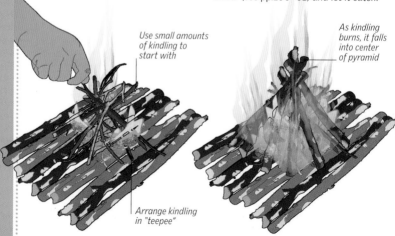

Use small amounts of kindling to start with

Arrange kindling in "teepee"

2 Gently lay kindling by the tinder ball. Build a kindling "teepee." This lets the fire breathe where the heat is strongest.

As kindling burns, it falls into center of pyramid

3 As the kindling catches fire and the flames grow, add larger pieces of kindling, slowly building up to split logs.

TYPE OF FIRE	HOW TO BUILD	WHY TO BUILD
TEEPEE	• Surround the tinder ball with kindling in the shape of a teepee. Arrange small, medium, and large fuel logs in a square at its foot	• Quick to light • Wet wood can be burned because it's dried by the heat of the inner fire
STONE-LINED	• Arrange large, non-porous stones in a circle, place a tinder ball in the middle, with kindling around it. Add fuel logs when the fire is established	• Stones shelter fire from wind • Using an existing fire ring reduces the fire's impact on the environment
AUTOMATIC	• Line a hole 3ft (1m) deep with non-porous stones. Put tinder and kindling inside and rest large logs against the sides so they drop down as they burn	• Self-feeding once lit, which means you don't need to keep adding fuel
LONG LOG	• Put tinder, kindling, and fuel logs in a depression 6ft (2m) long. Lay two long fuel logs on top of the burning fire	• Long-lasting (the fire can stay alight all night) • Emits a great deal of heat
SNAKE HOLE	• Create a hole in the side of a bank and a chimney up through the ground. Light a fire inside using any fuel	• Chimney creates a draft, giving a high-temperature fire • Sheltered from the elements
STAR-SHAPED	• Build a fire from tinder, kindling, and fuel • Arrange four logs so they meet in the middle • Push logs in as they burn	• Long-lasting • Good embers for cooking
HUNTER	• Make a fire out of tinder, kindling, and any type of fuel. Place two long logs either side of the fire in a V-shape	• Hardwood logs shelter the fire from the wind • Produces a great deal of heat
DAKOTA HOLE	• Dig a large hole for the fire and a slightly smaller hole for the chimney, with a tunnel linking the two. Use small logs as fuel • Cook at ground level	• Concentrated heat • Flames are below ground, so fire is hidden

Making sparks

Lighting tinder is the first stage of making a fire.
Matches and lighters do this instantly, but there are
also other ways of creating a spark that you can then
use to coax your tinder into a flame.

Ignition devices

There are various methods of creating
a spark. If you don't have matches or a lighter,
you'll need another device, such as a flint and
steel. You can also improvise by using an external
energy source. One way is to focus the sun's heat
with a magnifying glass. You can also make
sparks with a battery or create a chemical
reaction using potassium permanganate.

WARNING

Potassium permanganate
is a strong oxidizer that
can, when mixed with
certain chemicals, create
an explosive mixture. It
can also stain your skin
and clothes.

TYPE OF DEVICE	WHAT TO DO	POINTS TO NOTE
MATCHES/LIGHTERS	• To light a match "commando style," strike it away from you on the box and then cup it in your hands (see opposite).	• Waterproof matches are usually standard matches coated with wax and varnish. • Always have a lighter around your neck on a piece of cord.
MAGNIFYING GLASS	• Focus bright sunlight onto some dry tinder and create a hot spot. Hold the magnifying glass steady until the tinder catches alight.	• When you choose a compass, make sure it has a magnifying glass incorporated into it (to read details on maps). • You can also use the lens in reading glasses.
BATTERY/FLASHLIGHT	• Lay the wire across the battery terminals to create sparks. • Remove the bulb from the flashlight and place wire wool over the terminal. Switch on the flashlight to create sparks.	• The thinner the wire, the better this will work, especially with lower voltage batteries (1.5v). • Use this method for a short period only, otherwise you will drain the battery.

Striking a match

It may seem simple enough, but there's a way of striking a match—known as "commando style"—that reliably produces a flame in all kinds of conditions.

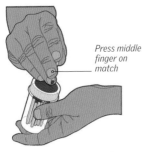

Press middle finger on match

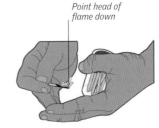

Point head of flame down

1 Hold the box in one hand and a match between the thumb and first two fingers of the other. Strike the match firmly, away from yourself.

2 When the match lights, cup your hands to protect the flame. Let the flame burn a little way along the stem before using it to light the tinder.

TYPE OF DEVICE	WHAT TO DO	POINTS TO NOTE
FIRESTEEL	• Hold the striker next to the tinder. • Place the firesteel directly onto the tinder, under the striker. • Draw the firesteel back across the striker to direct sparks onto the tinder. The firesteel moves, not the striker.	• This lasts for about 12,000 strikes. • The temperature reaches 5,400°F (3,000°C). • This works in all weathers and at any altitude. • A one-handed version of this is also available.
ONE-HANDED STRIKER	• Place the flint rod in the tinder. • Press the thumb button onto the rod and push the handle down the length of the rod. • Pushing the handle harder creates greater friction, which leads to a more intense spark.	• This works in all weathers. • A safety feature prevents accidental use. • It's designed for fighter pilots, who may injure an arm or hand after ejecting.
POTASSIUM PERMANGANATE	• Mix potassium permanganate and sugar in equal amounts on a hard surface. • Press down on the mixture with your knife and drag the blade along to create a spark.	• You can also mix a small amount of potassium permanganate with glycol or antifreeze. Quickly wrap it in paper and put it on the ground. **Warning:** stand clear; the combustion can be sudden and dangerous.

Extreme survival: in the desert

WHAT TO DO

ARE YOU IN DANGER?

If you are in a group, try to help any others who are in danger

◀ NO　　YES ▶

Get yourself out of it:
Sun/Heat—Find or improvise shelter immediately
Animals—Avoid confrontation and move away from danger
Injury—Stabilize condition and apply first aid

▶ **ASSESS YOUR SITUATION** ◀
See pp.154–57

▼

DOES ANYONE KNOW YOU WILL BE MISSING OR WHERE YOU ARE?

If no one knows you are missing or where you are, you must notify people of your plight by any means

◀ NO　　YES ▶

If you are missed, a rescue party will almost certainly be despatched to find you

▼

DO YOU HAVE ANY MEANS OF COMMUNICATION?

You are faced with surviving for an indefinite period—until you are located or you find help

◀ NO　　YES ▶

If you have a cell or satellite phone, let someone know your predicament. If your situation is serious enough for emergency rescue, and you have a Personal Locator Beacon (PLB), consider this option

▼

CAN YOU SURVIVE WHERE YOU ARE? *

If you cannot survive where you are and there are no physical reasons why you should remain, you will have to move to a location that offers a better chance of survival, rescue, or both

◀ NO　　YES ▶

Address the Principles of Survival: Protection; Location; Water; Food

YOU WILL HAVE TO MOVE **	YOU SHOULD STAY **

DO

- Make an informed decision on the best location to move to
- Leave clear indications of your intent (written messages or signs) if abandoning a vehicle
- Have aids to location accessible while moving and distributed when static
- Protect yourself against glare from the sun and windburn
- Seek or improvise shelter when not moving and seize all opportunities to collect fuel for a fire—deserts get cold at night
- Be on constant lookout for signs of water or civilization—such as green vegetation, converging animal/human tracks, or circling birds

DO

- Seek or improvise shade and work during the coolest part of the day/night. A shelter dug even 6in (15cm) below ground level will provide a much cooler place to rest
- Ration sweat, not water; you require around 1 quart (1 liter) per hour in temperatures above 100°F (38°C); half of this if it's cooler
- Continually reassess your water situation and options for augmenting your supplies
- Leave everything out overnight that could collect dew so you can drink it
- Prepare all of your aids to location for immediate use. Be constantly alert for signs of rescue

DON'T

- Sit directly on the hot ground when you stop
- Travel during the hottest part of the day
- Take risks—twisting an ankle by running down a sand dune could be fatal
- Force the pace—travel at the pace of the slowest person in the group
- Shelter in dry riverbeds, because of the potential risk of flash floods

DON'T

- Leave a broken down vehicle unless absolutely necessary—it's easier to see and is what rescuers will be looking for
- Waste energy—be idle unless there is something that must be done
- Ignore your fire—use anything that burns (such as wood and vehicle tires) to generate heat and smoke

* If you cannot survive where you are, but you also cannot move because of injury or other factors, you must do everything you can to attract rescue.

** If your situation changes (for instance, you are "moving" to find help, and you find a suitable location in which you can stay and survive) consult the alternative "Dos" and "Don'ts."

Making a bow drill

The bow drill set is one of the most efficient methods of making fire by friction. Try to find the right type of wood for each part, especially the drill and hearth board. This method requires knowledge, skill, practice, the correct wood, time, and effort.

TOOLS AND MATERIALS

- Knife
- Dry wood (see panel, opposite)
- Cordage such as paracord, fishing line, shoelaces, or bailing twine

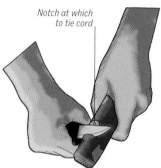

Notch at which to tie cord

1 For the bow, cut a stick as long as your arm, and cut a notch near each end. Tie cord with an arbor knot (see p.112) to one notch and with a double chain fastening knot (see p.113) to the other. Leave enough slack to wrap around your finger.

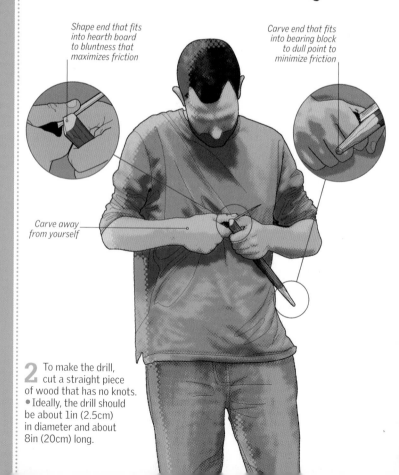

Shape end that fits into hearth board to bluntness that maximizes friction

Carve end that fits into bearing block to dull point to minimize friction

Carve away from yourself

2 To make the drill, cut a straight piece of wood that has no knots.
- Ideally, the drill should be about 1in (2.5cm) in diameter and about 8in (20cm) long.

Use knife point to make notch

3 Make the bearing block from hard wood about 3–4in (7.5–10cm) across. Cut it to a length of 4–5in (12–15cm), split it in two, and make a notch in it.

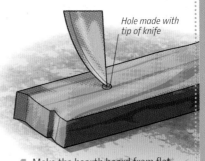

Hole made with tip of knife

4 Make the hearth board from flat wood about 1in (2.5cm) thick.
• Hold your drill so it sits about ³/₈in (1cm) from the edge of the board.
• Notch a small hole to help start the drill.

5 Set up the bow, drill, and bearing block (see p.106) and bow the drill into the hole in the hearth board until the hole is as wide as the drill. Don't go all the way through.

Twist cord once around drill, with cord on side of bow

Put drill's pointed end into hole

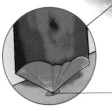

V should be about one-eighth of hole's circumference

6 Cut a V to the center of the hole through the hearth board. The bottom of this V is where the char collects and the ember forms in the ember pan (see p.106).

THE FINISHED FIRESET
The bow drill set works best when the drill and hearth board are made from the same dry wood, because both parts then wear down evenly.
• Good woods to start with are sycamore, hazel, ivy, lime, willow, and sotol (not found in Europe).
• Slight ridges or bumps on the drill will help prevent the cord from slipping.

BEARING BLOCK   DRILL   BOW

HEARTH BOARD

Using a bow drill

Before starting, have your dry tinder bundle, kindling, and fuel beside you. Initially, you will use lots of energy, so beware of overheating and dehydration. As much as possible, practice making tinder bundles and lighting them with a small coal from your camp fire.

Getting into position

Place the ember pan on a flat, dry surface and align it with the V on the hearth board. Loop the bow cord once around the drill, from the inside. Insert the drill into the hole on the hearth board, slot the block on top (with a green leaf in the notch for lubrication), and lock your wrist into your shin as support.

TOOLS AND MATERIALS

- Bow drill set (see pp.104–05)
- Thin, dry piece of bark to use as ember pan
- Buffed tinder, kindling, and fuel

Bear down on block with body weight

Keep head still above bow

Use arm for bowing

If drill slips, move grip farther along bow to increase tension in string

1 Hold the bow horizontal to the ground and parallel to your body.
- Lean forward and back to apply and reduce downward pressure to the drill.
- Start bowing slowly and evenly, using the full length of the bow. Breathing steadily, increase speed and pressure until smoke appears. Vigorously bow with maximum effort 10 more times—this usually produces a coal in the ember pan.

Keep drill upright

Steady hearth board with foot

Friction heats wood as drill turns

Black ash

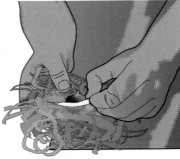

2 Gently remove the drill and lift the hearth board up, away from the coal.
• If the coal sticks to the board, tap the board with your knife to loosen it.
• Lift the ember pan off the ground and hold it in the air to see if the coal is glowing. If it is not glowing, but just smoking, gently fan it with your hand until you see it glow.

3 Transfer the coal into your tinder bundle. The coal must touch the tinder to transfer heat, so squeeze the tinder around the coal, but don't crush it or starve it of oxygen.

Air helps combustion

Hold tinder bundle up, away from face with your back to the wind

4 Gently blow into the bundle to help fan the coal and encourage it to catch.
• You can swing the bundle down and back up in between breaths to let dry air fan the coal.
• Continue as the amount of smoke increases and eventually, the bundle will burst into flames.

5 Don't throw the burning bundle on the ground; calmly place it where you intend to have your fire. Start building the fire around the bundle (see pp.98–99).

Once kindling is alight, add fuel

Use green wood as base

Man-made cordage

A vital piece of survival equipment, man-made cordage is a small item that has many uses: building a shelter, repairing equipment and clothing, making traps and nets, and producing fire using a bow drill. Pack plenty of it, both in your backpack and on your person, in case you get separated from your pack. Ensure the needle in your survival can has an eye big enough for the inner strands of the cordage.

PARACORD

This is a lightweight nylon rope made of 32 braided strands. Each strand has several smaller threads that can also be used. In most situations, this is a very good option, since it's readily available, strong, and packs down small.

USING CORDAGE

Always use your cordage efficiently. Tie simple, strong knots that can be released without cutting, to keep the cordage intact for the next task. In a survival situation, red is the ideal color because it stands out. Cut paracord into 30ft (10m) lengths, and tie them into coils or hanks, which you can keep in your pockets and pack.

OTHER TYPES OF CORDAGE

Before making cordage from natural materials (see opposite), see what else you might have that would be easier to adapt.

Shoelaces

For a ready supply of strong cordage, use twice as much shoelace as you need and wrap the extra length around the top of your boots before tying it.

Belts, clothing, and hats

You can cut any type of belt or clothing into strips. You can even use your hat—a 1in (2.5cm) strip from the brim of a jungle hat is just over 3ft (1m) long.

Raiding your kit

Possible items include guylines, draw cords, a towrope, or dental floss.

Be a scavenger

Collect anything that seems useful, from plastic bottles to bailing twine.

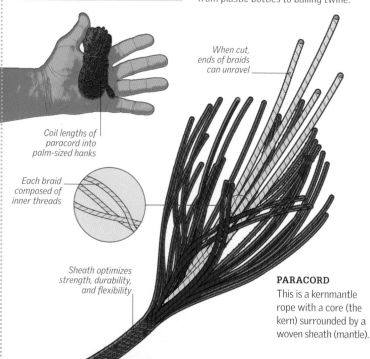

Coil lengths of paracord into palm-sized hanks

When cut, ends of braids can unravel

Each braid composed of inner threads

Sheath optimizes strength, durability, and flexibility

PARACORD

This is a kernmantle rope with a core (the kern) surrounded by a woven sheath (mantle).

Natural cordage

If you don't have man-made cordage, you can make a natural substitute. For example, use the roots and stems of plants to improvise a rope to erect shelters. Other possible raw materials include bark and sinews. Search your immediate environment to see what can be used.

Preparing nettle fibers

Old stinging nettles or wood nettles with long stems have the most fibers. Wearing gloves (or with your hands covered), strip the leaves from the nettles by grasping the stem at the base and pulling your clenched fist up the full length of the stem.

1 Sit astride a log and lay a nettle stem in front of you. Roll a smooth, rounded stick back and forth on the stem, pressing down hard, until the stem is crushed.

2 With your thumbnail, tease open the crushed tissue along the whole length of the stem. This exposes the spongy pith within.

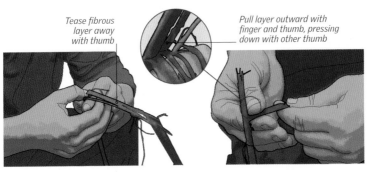

Tease fibrous layer away with thumb

Pull layer outward with finger and thumb, pressing down with other thumb

3 Bend the stem in the middle of its length. The inner pith will break away from the outer skin, making it easy for you to separate them.

4 Carefully peel the outer skin from the pith. The long, fibrous strips of skin can be made into short bindings or natural cordage (see p.110).

MAKING CORDAGE FROM PLANTS

Aside from having enough quantities of the plant material, ensure that it fulfills certain requirements.
- The fibers should be long enough. If you have to splice them together to make workable lengths, you will weaken the line.

- If braiding pieces together to make a stronger line, use rougher fibers, as they will bite together better. Shiny or smooth fibers tend to unravel easily.
- The fibers need to be strong and pliable enough so they don't break when you bend and tie them.

Making natural cordage

Once you have prepared a sufficient quantity of fibers (see p.109), let them dry before using them. However, in a survival situation you can use them before drying. Twisting the fibers is one of the most effective methods of making natural cordage. As with most survival tasks, practice makes perfect.

Twisted cordage

Start your first length of cordage closer to one end (not in the middle)—this offsets subsequent splices, which will provide strength, since splices are a potential weak point. If they are thin enough, the twisted cordage fibers can be braided to create a thicker cord that's even stronger.

TOOLS AND MATERIALS

• A sufficient quantity of prepared natural fibers (see p.109) to give you the length of cordage that you require.

❝ IN ORDER TO **DRY THE FIBERS**, HANG THEM UP **IN THE SUN** OR **NEAR A FIRE**. ❞

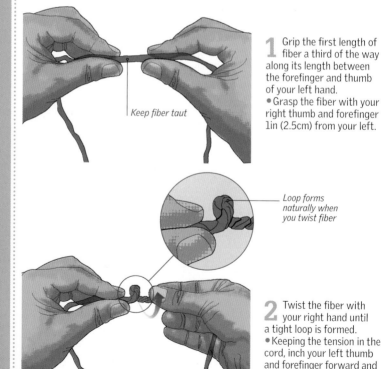

Keep fiber taut

1 Grip the first length of fiber a third of the way along its length between the forefinger and thumb of your left hand.
• Grasp the fiber with your right thumb and forefinger 1in (2.5cm) from your left.

Loop forms naturally when you twist fiber

2 Twist the fiber with your right hand until a tight loop is formed.
• Keeping the tension in the cord, inch your left thumb and forefinger forward and clamp down on the loop.

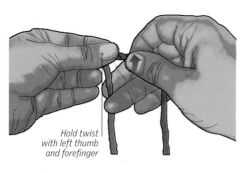

3 Move your right hand back so that 1in (2.5cm) of cord is visible, and apply another twist.
• At the same time, grasp the left-hand cord with the middle and fourth fingers of the right hand.

Hold twist with left thumb and forefinger

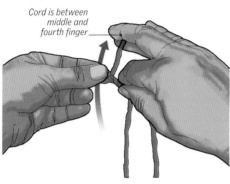

Cord is between middle and fourth finger

4 Sweep the middle and fourth fingers of your right hand upward, pulling the left-hand cord under the captive piece.
• Inch your left thumb and forefinger forward, clamping down on the new twist.

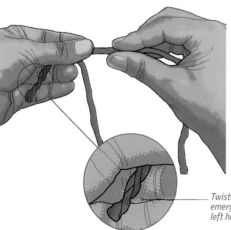

5 You can now release your right thumb and forefinger, letting the lower cord fall.
• Grip the upper cord 1in (2.5cm) from your left fingers with your right thumb and forefinger.

Twisted cordage emerges in left hand

6 Repeat Steps 3, 4, and 5 as you proceed along the length of cord.
• To splice in an extra length, overlap the new piece 2in (5cm) along the existing one and twist the two together between your left thumb and forefinger. Then, continue as before.

Arbor knot

This knot has several survival uses. If you erect a poncho or a tarp (see pp.78–91), it can secure one end of a line to a fixed point, where no adjustment is needed. It can also secure two poles together—for instance, in an A-frame shelter (see p.81).

(see pp.78–91)
(see p.81)

THE ENDS OF A LINE

The end that takes the most active part in knot-tying is the working end. The more passive end is called the standing end, around which the knot is tied.

Working line passes over standing line

Hold point where both lines cross

1 With the working end in your right hand and the standing line in your left, pass the cord around the tree.
• Loop the working end over the standing line, then back and over the cord around the tree.

Tie overhand knot around standing line

2 Pass the working end around the standing line, and then over itself to form an overhand loop.
• Pass the free end up through the loop. (You have now tied an overhand knot around the standing line).

3 Keep the standing line taut with your left hand. Pull the working end down with your right.
• By pulling on the working end, you will tighten the overhand knot around the standing line.

Pull to unlock

Two single overhand knots tightly locked

4 Tie another overhand knot in the working end, as close to the first knot as possible.
• Pull on the standing line to lock the two knots together. Then, give the standing line a sharp tug.

Double chain fastening knot

This knot securely attaches the free end of a line to a fixture, particularly when weight is involved and you don't want the knot to slip or come loose.

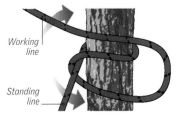

Working line

Standing line

1 Loop the working end around the fixture, such as a tree or pole. Pass it over and around the standing line.

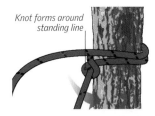

Knot forms around standing line

2 Pass the working end back around the fixture and then bring it back under the standing line.

3 Pass the working end over the top and around the standing line again, and once more around the fixture.

Working line goes through

4 Bringing the working line around, thread it under itself to complete the knot. Lock the knot into position.

Slip knot

This is a good example of a simple knot with many practical uses in survival situations.

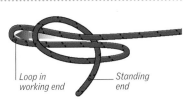

Loop in working end

Standing end

2 Make a loop with the working end and pass it into the first loop.
• Collect the second loop with your left thumb and forefinger and pull it through.

Hold working end between right thumb and forefinger

Hold standing end between left thumb and forefinger

1 Twist the standing line over the working line to form a loop. Hold this loop between your left thumb and forefinger.

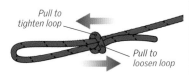

Pull to tighten loop

Pull to loosen loop

3 With your right thumb and forefinger, pull both ends away from the loop in your left hand. Put the loop over whatever you want to secure. Pull the knot tight.

Siberian hitch

Also known as the "Evenk knot," this is a good knot for attaching a rope to a fixture—for example, when securing a ridgeline to a tree for a poncho shelter (see p.79).

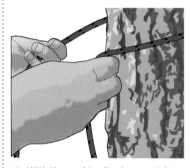

1 With the working line in your right hand and the standing line in your left, pass the cord around the tree.

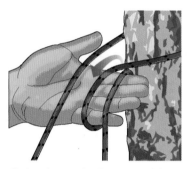

2 Lay the standing line on your left palm. Loop the working line one and a half times around your fingers.

3 Bring your left hand under the standing line.
• Turn the palm of your hand so that one loop twists over another.

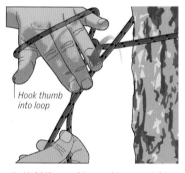

Hook thumb into loop

4 Hold the working end in your right thumb and forefinger.
• Bring the loop that is around your left fingers over the standing line.

5 Pinch the working line with your left-hand fingers. Pull it up through the loop to tighten the knot on itself.

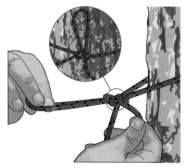

6 Pull the working end to tighten the knot around the tree. To free the knot, pull the end of the standing line.

Taut line hitch

This knot is widely used in survival and outdoor activities, since it can be adjusted to increase or decrease the tension in a fixed line—for example, a guy-line on a tent or a mooring on a boat in tidal waters.

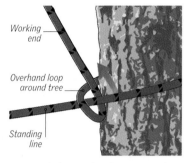

Working end

Overhand loop around tree

Standing line

1 Attach the standing line to an anchor point. Form a loop with the working line and pass the working end through it.

2 Pass the working end up through the loop again so the two knots sit side by side. Don't tighten them yet.

3 Pass the working end under the standing line and back through the loop it created (outside the earlier loops).

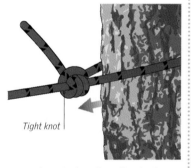

Tight knot

4 Tighten the knot by pulling both the lines. Pull the knot farther from the anchor point to increase the tension.

QUICK-RELEASE KNOT
You can dismantle a tent or free a boat from its mooring more quickly by finishing off the taut line hitch (above) with a quick-release knot.

Bight in working line

1 Repeat Step 3 of the taut line hitch, but make a loop (bight) in the working line and pass it—rather than just the end—through the loop.

2 Tighten the knot as in Step 4 of the taut line hitch. Leave the working end free so you can pull it quickly to release the knot.

Using a knife

Anyone venturing into the wilderness should carry some kind of knife, preferably a bushcraft knife. It is probably the most important survival tool, after knowledge.

Bushcraft knife

An experienced person can accomplish most survival skills, such as making feather sticks (see p.95), with a bushcraft knife. This knife has a number of features that will help you in every situation.

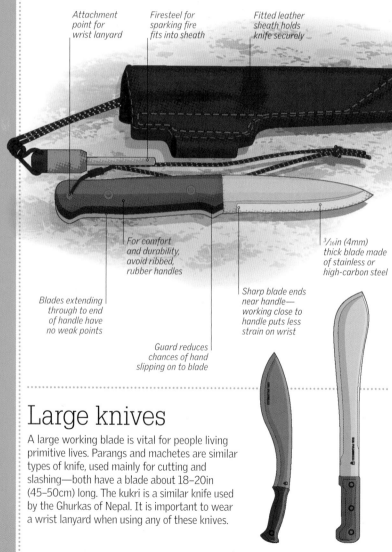

Attachment point for wrist lanyard

Firesteel for sparking fire fits into sheath

Fitted leather sheath holds knife securely

For comfort and durability, avoid ribbed, rubber handles

Blades extending through to end of handle have no weak points

Sharp blade ends near handle—working close to handle puts less strain on wrist

Guard reduces chances of hand slipping on to blade

$^3/_{16}$in (4mm) thick blade made of stainless or high-carbon steel

Large knives

A large working blade is vital for people living primitive lives. Parangs and machetes are similar types of knife, used mainly for cutting and slashing—both have a blade about 18–20in (45–50cm) long. The kukri is a similar knife used by the Ghurkas of Nepal. It is important to wear a wrist lanyard when using any of these knives.

KUKRI   MACHETE/PARANG

Working with your knife

How you hold your bushcraft knife can help you in various cutting tasks. Some essential grips include the forehand, backhand, and chest lever. Usually, you need to grip the handle at the end nearest to the blade so you can cut with the part of the blade nearest to the handle.

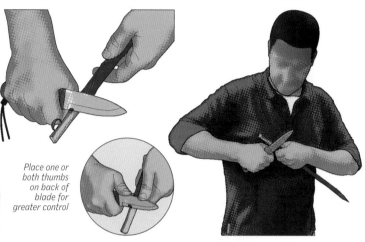

Place one or both thumbs on back of blade for greater control

FOREHAND GRIP
This most natural and common grip allows your back and arm to provide strength, while your wrist provides control. Ensure that the blade is facing down.

CHEST LEVER
Hold the knife in a backhand grip, using your arm and chest muscles to provide power. You can cut close to your body while your wrists control the action.

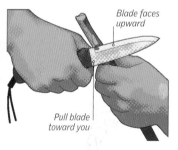

Blade faces upward

Pull blade toward you

BACKHAND GRIP
Use this grip when you want to see and control exactly where the blade is going, or if the follow-through after cutting would injure you.

SAFELY PASSING A KNIFE
A group may only have one good knife for everyone to use, so you may need to pass it around frequently. For safety, pass the knife handle first, with the blade up.

KNIFE KNOW-HOW
- A bushcraft knife is used for carving, cutting, and splitting small logs. For chopping large logs, use either a machete or a saw.
- A knife doesn't need to be longer than 8–9in (20–22.5cm).
- When working with wood, don't use a knife with a serrated edge, since this makes it hard to use the part of the blade closest to the handle.
- Clean and dry the blade when not in use, and return it to its sheath.
- Wear your sheath on your belt or around your neck on a lanyard.

Finding Water and Food

Finding Water and Food

The importance of water, even in a short-term survival situation, should never be underestimated. Water is essential to life, and a regular intake of 2–3 quarts (2–3 liters) a day is needed just to maintain your water balance and prevent dehydration. The amount required can increase dramatically, depending on factors such as the temperature of the environment, your age and physical condition, your workload, and whether you have been injured. It's not unusual for soldiers operating in desert or jungle environments to require $3^1/_2$ gallons (14 liters) per day.

Plan your treks around your need for water and your ability to replace it as required. You should always strive to filter and purify any water before drinking it. There are many hydration systems available, and many small and efficient methods of filtering and purifying water on the trail. In the short-term, stomach bugs from contaminated water may not kill you but they can seriously affect your ability to perform other survival tasks. However, if you have no choice, it's better to drink contaminated water than not to drink at all. That way, a doctor will at least be able to treat you, whereas dehydration will kill you. Never drink urine or salt water, since these will only dehydrate you more.

In a short-term survival situation, food should not be your major priority. While you may go through food withdrawal symptoms, you're not going to die of starvation within a few days. However, hunger, a lack of energy, and deterioration in coordination can be expected after a few days. If the opportunity to procure food arises, eat little and often, but make sure you have sufficient water to digest it.

In a long-term survival situation, your survival priorities will change and the need for food in order to survive will become more important. There is a thin line between food not being a priority and then subsequently finding that you're in no physical condition to do anything about it when it does become a priority—regularly reassess your situation and alter your plans accordingly. It takes knowledge, effort, skill, and a certain amount of luck to obtain food in the wild.

Finding food

Your body converts food into fuel. It provides you with heat and energy, and helps you recover from work, injury, or sickness. A healthy body can survive for weeks without food, using reserves stored in its tissues. You will use approximately 70 calories per hour just breathing; and up to 5,500 calories per day if working hard.

When gathering food in the wild, always ensure that the energy gained from the food is more than the energy expended in procuring it; otherwise, it's a wasteful exercise.

Food that's easy to find, gather, and prepare should always be your first priority:
• Plants are easy to collect and, as long as they're readily available in the environment you're in, should be your first choice for food. However, you should be absolutely sure that they are edible—mistakenly eating the wrong leaf or berry could cause vomiting and diarrhea, making your situation worse. Avoid mushrooms unless you are 100% sure they are edible—mushrooms can kill!
• Fishing requires little effort once the lines or traps have been set, and they will work for you around the clock. Fish is high in protein and relatively simple to prepare and cook.
• Insects, reptiles, and amphibians may also be available. Remember, however, that many are poisonous, although they can be used as bait for fish and mammals.
• Birds and mammals have their own survival mechanisms and are wary of humans, especially in remote areas where contact with humans is limited. Even if caught, the bird or mammal will need to be killed, plucked or skinned, and cooked.

The importance of water

You require a steady supply of water to sustain yourself in a survival situation and without it you will dehydrate. Left unchecked, dehydration will end in death. To survive, a balance between water intake and loss must exist.

Why you need water

Water is needed, directly or indirectly, for every physical and chemical process occuring in your body. Here are a few functions that water performs:

- **Delivery service:** water carries oxygen, nutrients, and other essentials around the body.
- **Waste remover:** the kidneys use water to flush out toxins and waste matter via urine.
- **Coolant:** water regulates your body temperature.

- **Breathing aid:** the lungs use water to moisten inhaled air so that it doesn't irritate the sensitive pulmonary linings.
- **Sensory aid:** water helps conduct nervous impulses around the body.
- **Shock absorber:** water protects the vital organs and provides lubrication around the joints.

What is dehydration?

Dehydration occurs when you fail to replace the water your body loses. Possible factors include high and low temperatures, humidity, work rate, clothing, body size, fitness levels, and injury.

THE EFFECTS OF WATER LOSS		
1–5% LOST	6–10% LOST	11–12% LOST
Thirst	Dizziness	Stiffness of joints
Discomfort	Dry mouth	Deafness
Darkened urine	Blueness of extremities	Defective vision
Loss of appetite	Slurred speech	Shriveled skin
Impatience	Swollen tongue	Lack of feeling in skin
Drowsiness	Blurred vision	Inability to swallow
Lethargy	Tingling in limbs	Delirium
Nausea	Inability to walk	Unconsciousness
Headache	Difficulty in breathing	Death

The functions of water

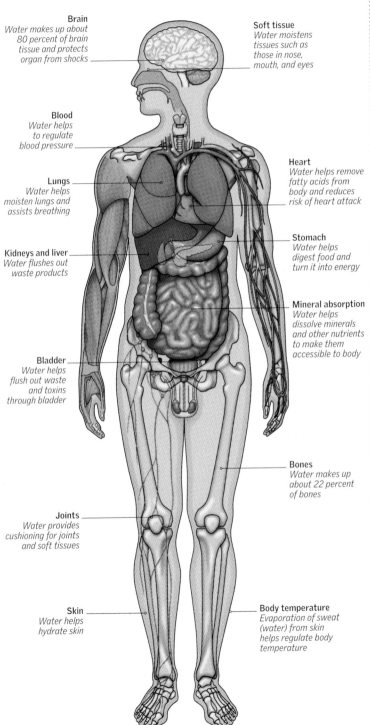

Brain
Water makes up about 80 percent of brain tissue and protects organ from shocks

Soft tissue
Water moistens tissues such as those in nose, mouth, and eyes

Blood
Water helps to regulate blood pressure

Heart
Water helps remove fatty acids from body and reduces risk of heart attack

Lungs
Water helps moisten lungs and assists breathing

Stomach
Water helps digest food and turn it into energy

Kidneys and liver
Water flushes out waste products

Mineral absorption
Water helps dissolve minerals and other nutrients to make them accessible to body

Bladder
Water helps flush out waste and toxins through bladder

Bones
Water makes up about 22 percent of bones

Joints
Water provides cushioning for joints and soft tissues

Skin
Water helps hydrate skin

Body temperature
Evaporation of sweat (water) from skin helps regulate body temperature

Water-borne disease

Water-borne diseases are caused by ingesting water contaminated by the feces or urine of humans or animals, which contain protozoa, viruses, bacteria, or intestinal parasites. Globally, these diseases cause 10 million deaths a year.

	DISEASE	SYMPTOMS
PROTOZOA	Cryptosporidium	Loss of appetite, nausea, and abdominal pain, usually followed by profuse, foul-smelling, watery diarrhea, and vomiting.
PROTOZOA	Giardiasis	Loss of appetite, lethargy, fever, vomiting, diarrhea, blood in the urine, and abdominal cramps.
VIRUS	Infectious hepatitis (Hepatitis A)	Nausea, loss of appetite, mild fever, aching muscles, dark-colored urine, jaundice, and abdominal pain.
BACTERIUM	Amebic dysentery	Feeling of fatigue and listlessness. Feces may be solid, but will smell foul and contain blood and mucus.
BACTERIUM	Bacillary dysentery (Shigellosis)	Fever, abdominal pain, muscle cramps, high temperature, and blood, pus, and mucus in stools.
BACTERIUM	Cholera	Vomiting, poor circulation, cold and clammy skin, muscle cramps, rapid dehydration, and increased heart-rate.
BACTERIUM	E. coliform	Diarrhea and vomiting. Can cause death in vulnerable groups such as the very young or the elderly.
BACTERIUM	Leptospirosis	Jaundiced appearance, lethargy, high temperature, aching muscles, and vomiting. Can be fatal if not diagnosed early.
BACTERIUM	Salmonella	Nausea, diarrhea, headaches, stomach cramps, fever, possible blood in the feces, and vomiting.
PARASITES	Bilharzia	Irritation to the urinary tract and blood in urine, rash or itchy skin, abdominal pain, cough, diarrhea, fever, and fatigue.
PARASITES	Hookworms	Anemia and lethargy. Larvae travel to lungs and are coughed up and swallowed into the stomach, where they grow into worms.

" IN THE **FIRST 24 HOURS** OF A SURVIVAL SITUATION, YOU'LL BE ADDRESSING THE PRINCIPLES OF SURVIVAL: **PROTECTION AND LOCATION**. THIS IS HARD, **THIRSTY WORK**. "

Q | HOW MUCH WATER DO I NEED?

A | The amount of water you need to survive a particular situation depends on various factors, such as your physical state, the environment you are in, and your exertion level. Even when resting in the shade, an average person will lose more than 1 quart (1 liter) of water each day just through breathing and urination, a figure that increases dramatically once loss of water through sweat is taken into account. A minimum of 3 quarts (3 liters) per day is required to remain healthy in a survival situation, with this amount increasing for higher temperatures and heavier workloads.

Q | HOW MUCH WATER IS TOO MUCH?

A | Hyponatremia is a condition caused when excess water accumulates in the body at a higher rate than it can be excreted. It results in a diminished sodium concentration in the plasma and the swelling of the cells. It can lead to a swollen brain and other neurological problems and, in extreme cases, coma and death. The way to prevent the condition is to control your water and salt intake. If you don't have salt or sodium tablets in your survival kit, you can filter saltwater through fabric to sift out the salt content.

Q | HOW DO I RATION MY WATER?

A | If your water supplies are limited, you'll have to efficiently use what rations you have until you're rescued. If your water rations will not last that long, you'll have to procure water yourself. There is much debate about the advantages and disadvantages of drinking no water for the first 24 hours of a survival situation, but at this early stage it's best to make sure you're adequately hydrated. Your particular circumstances will dictate what's best to do, but always consider the following:

• The incident that put you in the survival situation may have been both dramatic and stressful; this will make you thirsty.

• In the first 24 hours of a survival situation, you'll be addressing the principles of survival: protection (shelter) and location (see pp.20–21). This is hard, thirsty work.

• Physical factors—such as seasickness, injury, or the environment you're in, such as a desert—may dictate that water-rationing is not a viable option.

• If you only have a limited water supply, but drink nothing for the first 24 hours, you may end up being so dehydrated that what little water you have in your possession will have no positive effect on your dehydrated state.

Finding water: temperate climates

You can find water in a range of sources—locate the best and most accessible source of water in your immediate environment.

Catching rainwater

Collecting rain as it falls is the safest way to procure drinking water. It will need no treatment prior to drinking, as long as the catchment device itself has not been contaminated. Any non-porous material can be used as a rain-catchment device.

Collect rainwater in tarp as it falls

Use sticks as stakes

Stone weight to create natural run-off point

Container to catch rainwater

TOOLS AND MATERIALS

- Tarpaulin
- Four sticks
- String
- Heavy stone
- Container

1 Select a place as close to your camp as possible, where your catchment device will be exposed to the most possible rain.

2 Secure the tarp to four stakes. Ensure one end is higher than the other to provide a run-off for the water.

3 Place a stone in the middle of the device, about two-thirds of the way toward the lower end, to create a channel into which the rain will run down.

4 Place a container, such as a mess can, below the end of the channel to collect the water as it starts to flow off the tarp.

Other natural water sources

If rainwater is not available, there may be other natural sources of water, from visible streams to hidden bores and holes. Whatever your source, you should always treat the water before drinking it.

SOURCE	CHARACTERISTICS
SPRINGS	These occur when water is forced to the surface due to subterranean pressures or gravitational flow from higher sources. They provide a permanent water source in low-lying areas. Contrasting green vegetation indicates their presence.
STREAMS AND RIVERS	The closer to the mountaintop the river or stream is, the clearer the fast-running water will be. Either check upstream for contaminants, or follow the water downstream. Collect the fast-flowing water near to the surface.
ROCK HOLES	Usually found in high ground, rock holes are natural collectors of rainwater. If the water appears to be trapped deep down, you can use your surgical tubing to retrieve it.
WELLS AND BORES	Wells, which may be featured on local maps, can be deep and covered. In remote areas, wells are covered and marked in certain ways by the locals—find out what the markers are for your area.
LAKES AND PONDS	Rivers, streams, and water run-offs all flow into lakes or ponds. Collect water as it runs into the water body, as static water becomes increasingly stagnant.
SEEPAGE	Usually located at the base of cliffs or rocky outcrops, seepage is caused by slow-running channels that drain off these features.
SOAKS	Soaks are found close to rivers and creeks in low-lying areas, and are normally lower than the existing water table. Their presence is often indicated by vegetation and they may be subject to pollution due to their use by animals.

AVOIDING POTENTIAL DANGERS

Most water sources are likely to be used by animals for drinking, bathing, urinating, and defecating, so always filter and purify any water collected before use (see pp.144–47); the only exception to this rule is rainwater. When collecting water, you should also be aware of certain dangers. You may encounter dangerous animals either using the water source, or on the way either to or from it. Most major water sources have a ranking system to determine which animals can use it. If all of the small gazelles suddenly disappear, ask yourself why. If you're collecting water from rivers, consider the potential dangers of river wildlife. If using dry riverbeds during the rainy season, be aware that flash floods can move quicker than you can run.

IN ARID AREAS, RIVERS AND STREAMS TEND ONLY TO **FLOW DURING FLOODS** AND WILL CONTAIN MORE POLLUTANTS.

Sourcing water from dew

Dew is water droplets that form on exposed surfaces in early morning or late evening. It can provide an invaluable supply of fresh water. It occurs when the temperature of a surface is low enough to allow the moisture in the warmer air above it to condense. Dew can easily be collected from any non-porous surface—such as a car roof or a tarpaulin—with a piece of cloth that can then be wrung out into a container. You can also harvest or trap dew.

HARVESTING DEW

You can harvest dew by walking through a field of long grass before sunrise or late in the evening, with a piece of absorbent material—such as rags or a T-shirt—tied around your ankles.

1 Tie the material tightly around each ankle and walk through the dew-covered grass. It will absorb the dew as you move.

2 Wring the rags to extract the water. Repeat the process until you have an ample supply of water or the dew has evaporated.

MAKING A DEW TRAP

Dig a hole about 18in (45cm) deep, line with a plastic sheet, and fill it with smooth, clean stones. Water will condense on the stones overnight. Harvest as early as possible the next morning to ensure it does not evaporate.

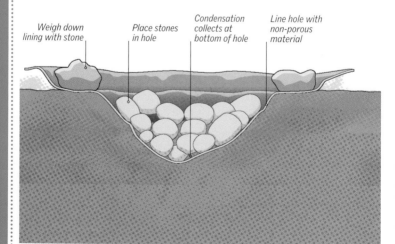

Weigh down lining with stone

Place stones in hole

Condensation collects at bottom of hole

Line hole with non-porous material

Sourcing water from plants

Transpiration is the evaporation of water from a plant, primarily from its leaves. You can collect this vapor to boost your fresh water supply. All you need is a clear plastic bag.

MAKING A VEGETATION BAG

Cut green vegetation and place it in a plastic bag. Place a smooth rock in the lower corner of the bag, and tie off the open end. Secure the bag in direct sunlight so that water in the leaves evaporates and condensation forms.

DELAYING DEHYDRATION

The following points will help you delay the onset of dehydration:
• Conserve what water you have and use it as efficiently as possible.
• Work only in the coolest part of the day and avoid sweating.
• If the Sun is shining, seek shade and keep covered.
• Suck a small, smooth button or pebble to help stimulate saliva and remove the sensation of thirst.
• Avoid eating protein-rich food, as it requires more water to digest than those in other food groups.

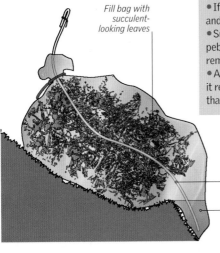

Fill bag with succulent-looking leaves

Retrieve water from bag with surgical tubing

Water collects in lower corner of bag

MAKING A TRANSPIRATION BAG

Place a smooth rock in the lower corner of the plastic bag, and place the bag over the leaves of a tree branch, tying the end. As water evaporates from the leaves, it will condense and collect at the bag's lowest point.

Making a solar still

A solar still works using the same principle as a vegetation bag (see p.129). It collects potable water from the vapor that is produced by vegetation, water that is unfit to drink, or moisture from the ground.

Surgical tubing to retrieve water

Small stone forms drip point on underside of plastic

Fabric soaked in undrinkable water or urine

Plastic sheet

Container catches condensed water droplets

Container holding undrinkable water or urine

1 Find, or dig, a hole in the ground at least 2ft (0.6m) wide and 2ft (0.6m) deep. Place an empty container in its center. Fill the hole with vegetation, a receptacle containing undrinkable water, such as saltwater or urine, or fabric soaked in undrinkable water.

2 Cover the hole with a plastic sheet. Place a stone in the center of the sheet to create a run-off point for the water. The Sun's heat will evaporate water from the vegetation, or distill the undrinkable water, producing pure water vapor. This vapor will condense on the underside of the plastic sheet, and drip into the container.

LOCATING HIDDEN WATER SOURCES

The presence of water is usually indicated by signs of life, such as green vegetation, animal tracks, or human habitation. Even if the terrain you're in appears lifeless, there may be plenty of indicators of a possible water source.

USE THE TERRAIN

- Observe the landscape for patches of green. Be aware that vegetation may not need obvious surface water for survival and may get its water from deep roots that tap into moisture below the surface.
- Water is more likely to be found downhill or in low-lying areas, such as valleys and at the base of cliffs or rock formations.
- Water will often seep inland on coastlines, leaving behind wetlands that contain water with tolerable levels of salt or that can be distilled in a solar still (see opposite).

WATCH THE ANIMALS

- The Bedouin listen to the twittering of birds at dawn and dusk, and follow their flight path to discover where they drink.
- Flocks of birds circling over one spot are usually flying over a water source. This does not apply to meat-eating birds, such as vultures.
- All finches and grain-eaters need a regular supply of water. Observe their flight patterns to locate a water source.
- Animal tracks often lead to a water source. Look for converging sets of tracks.
- The presence of flies, bees, and mosquitoes almost certainly means water is nearby.
- Look out for herd animals, such as elephants and wildebeest, because they depend on water.

Stones hold plastic sheet in position

THE SUN'S HEAT WILL EVAPORATE UNDRINKABLE WATER, PRODUCING WATER VAPOR THAT IS FREE OF CONTAMINANTS.

Finding water: hot-humid climates

Your need for water increases in hot climates as your body uses more of its water supply to regulate its temperature through perspiration. If you fail to drink more than you perspire, you will start to dehydrate. Hot climates can be divided into two groups: hot-humid and hot-dry. The hot-humid conditions found in jungles and rainforests make procuring water easy. However, you may have to drink up to $3^1/_2$ gallons (14 liters) a day to avoid dehydration.

Catching rainwater

Catching rainwater is the best way to procure water: it is passive and requires no energy to collect once you place your containers. There are many forms of catchment device, but make sure you filter and purify the water (see pp.144–47) before drinking it.

BAMBOO ROOF

Construct a sloped bamboo roof with a bamboo gutter. This could be the roof of your shelter, but if water procurement is a problem, you will have to construct additional bamboo roofs.

BAMBOO DRAINPIPE

Observe rainwater's route down a tree trunk and tie a length of bamboo cut in half lengthwise in its path. Place the other end of the bamboo into a container.

WIDE-LEAF ROOF

If there are wide-leafed plants around you, it's easy to construct a roof from them. Overlay the leaves as you would with roof tiles, working from the bottom to the top. They will allow the water to run to the bottom. Place a length of bamboo, cut in half lengthwise, as a collection gutter at the bottom.

WARNING

Water sources are plentiful in jungle and rainforest environments, and under normal circumstances, you should have no problem getting hold of enough water to satisfy your needs. However, rivers and streams may not be available during certain seasons, or if you have climbed too high, so knowledge of other water procurement methods could be crucial to your survival.

DRIP RAGS

Wrapping any absorbent material around a leaning tree, such as a rag or a T-shirt, will result in the water running down the tree and soaking the material. Shape the rag to form a low point from which water will drip, and place a suitable container underneath to catch the water.

" LIFE-SAVING FLUID IS EVERYWHERE IN THE JUNGLE, AND YOU DON'T HAVE TO LOOK FAR TO FIND IT. "

Sourcing water from vegetation

Many plants, such as pitcher plants, have hollow parts that collect rainfall or dew. Some trees store and catch rainwater in natural receptacles, such as cracks or hollows. In an emergency, life-saving liquid can be garnered from a tree's roots or sap. You can find water trapped in the sections of green bamboo by carefully cutting into the bamboo with your machete or knife; or collect small, unripe coconuts and quench your thirst with the fluid they contain; or make a spigot and tap into the water contained inside the tree.

WATER VINES

Found throughout the jungles and rainforests of tropical regions, water vines are easily identifiable by their size and shape; and can provide an excellent sort of fresh water. However, bear in mind that not all water vines are water-bearing; not all contain drinkable water, and some even contain poisonous sap.

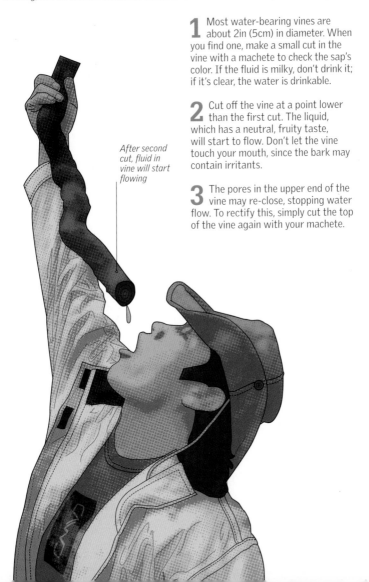

After second cut, fluid in vine will start flowing

1 Most water-bearing vines are about 2in (5cm) in diameter. When you find one, make a small cut in the vine with a machete to check the sap's color. If the fluid is milky, don't drink it; if it's clear, the water is drinkable.

2 Cut off the vine at a point lower than the first cut. The liquid, which has a neutral, fruity taste, will start to flow. Don't let the vine touch your mouth, since the bark may contain irritants.

3 The pores in the upper end of the vine may re-close, stopping water flow. To rectify this, simply cut the top of the vine again with your machete.

Finding water: hot-dry climates

Anyone venturing into this environment should have sufficient water for their needs, plus an emergency supply just in case. Green vegetation usually signifies water or moisture in some form, and many techniques of procuring water in temperate climates (see pp.126–31) may work in some desert conditions.

Sources of emergency fluid

If you find no surface water, and you have no other means of procuring water, a water-yielding plant may be your only option. In some plants, the clear sap, fruit, or trapped rainwater may quench your immediate thirst, but do not rely on these sources to keep you alive for long.

FINDING UNDERGROUND WATER

Unusual clusters of green plants may indicate a minor presence of water; an abundance of greenery may indicate a more substantial water source. Water is rarely found above a depth of 6ft (1.8m) below the surface, so you will have to dig for it. Make sure you only do so during the coolest part of the day. Remember that your chances of procuring water from the inside bend of a dry wadi in a real survival situation are slim.

> **THINK LATERALLY**
>
> If you have to procure water in the desert, chances are you'll already be in a desperate situation. Knowledge of the techniques outlined in the temperate environment section, (see pp.126–31) along with those mentioned here, could be enough to keep you alive in the desert.

PRICKLY PEARS

Found in low-spreading clumps measuring 3ft (0.9m) in height, and native to dry, sandy soils throughout the world, the prickly pear cactus has an edible fruit that can provide a life-saving amount of fluid.

Remove prickly outer layer of fruit before consumption

CHECKLIST FOR HOT-DRY CLIMATES

Many problems encountered in a desert environment can be avoided with some prior preparation.
• Always start hydrated.
• Carry enough water for your needs plus emergency water; your emergency supply should be enough to get you out of danger.
• Cache water ahead if necessary.
• Check your map for probable water sources. Confirm the reliability of these sources with locals and ask if there are any sources, such as wells, that are not shown on the map.

• Monitor your progress against the water you use. If you're using more than you thought, reevaluate what you want to accomplish. It's better to turn back and learn from a mistake than to push on and create a survival situation that need not exist.
• Mark your map, or waypoint your GPS, with any water sources you sight as you progress. It's better to go back to a known source than to move on with nothing more than hope.
• To keep the water cool, always keep the bottles in the shade or in a windy location.

Large clusters of thick, fleshy leaves around large central stalk

AGAVES

Native to Mexico and the southern and western United States, agaves have a rosette of thick, fleshy leaves containing fluid that is safe to drink. Cut the huge flower stalk with a knife or machete and collect the juice.

Numerous ribs and hundreds of sharp spines

BARREL-SHAPED CACTUS

Barrel-shaped cacti contain a milky fluid that's safe to drink. Carefully remove the top of the cactus with a machete, mash up the flesh inside with a stick to make a pulp, and extract the juice from the pulp by sucking through a hollow grass stem. Alternatively, use a cloth to soak up as much of the fluid as possible and then wring the material to extract the fluid. The rewards from both techniques are minimal.

Finding water: cold climates

Adopt the same methods as for temperate climates (see pp.126–31), although the ability to procure water becomes a problem in freezing temperatures. If you have a choice between melting ice and snow, favor ice, since it melts faster, and is much denser. If you can't find ice, use compact snow.

Melting ice

If you already have some water, pour it into a container and heat it over a fire. Break the ice into small pieces and add them to the container to melt them. Keep the water hot, but not boiling, so as not to lose water through evaporation.

USING A HOT PLATFORM

If you don't have water, you can melt ice slowly on a gently sloping platform fashioned from any flat piece of stone or wood positioned above a fire.

1 Build a fire. Search for a large stone with a flat surface, and two logs, or smaller stones strong enough to support it. Place the logs or stones on either side of the fire to support the large stone. Set the platform at an angle to create a natural runoff for the melting ice. Place an ice block in the center of the platform.

Collect meltwater in mess can as it flows off platform

2 As the fire starts to heat up the platform, the ice will begin to melt. The meltwater will flow off the platform, where it can be collected in a container.

CHECKLIST FOR COLD CLIMATES

Prioritize water usage in cold weather in the same manner as you would in the desert (see pp.134–35).

• Find a water source close to everything you need to build and maintain a fire.

• Look for an alternative water source before trying to melt snow or ice. It's more time- and fuel-efficient to fill your water container with natural meltwater.

• Your ability to procure water in freezing conditions will be directly related to your ability to start and maintain a fire.

• You'll need enough fuel to maintain a fire for a considerable period of time.

• Regulate your body heat to minimize overheating and sweating.

• Keep drinking water close to your body to prevent it from freezing, but avoid having containers directly next to your skin. Keep them between layers of clothing and use the warmer air trapped between the layers, since this will help raise the water's temperature.

• Do not use recently frozen seawater, because it contains high levels of salt.

Block of ice in center of platform

Set platform on gentle slope to let water run off

Support platform on two logs

Light small fire to heat platform and melt ice

WARNING

Never try to melt ice or snow in your mouth, because it can cause freezing injuries to your mouth and lips. What's more, your body will expend heat as it melts the ice, which could lead to hypothermia.

Melting snow

If you already have water, follow the techniques for melting ice (see p.136), heating a little water and adding bits of snow. Don't pack the snow too tightly; if an air pocket forms, the heat from the fire will be absorbed by the metal container rather than by the snow and could result in the fire burning a hole through the metal container before it melts the snow.

STORING WATER

Snow is a great insulator: even if the temperature dips to -40°F (-40°C), water in a bottle will remain largely unfrozen if placed under at least 1ft (0.3m) of snow. Make sure you store the bottles upside-down. That way, if some of the water does freeze, it will freeze at the bottom of the bottle and not at the top.

❝ ALWAYS LOOK FOR THE **WHITEST, PUREST-LOOKING** SNOW, AND **ICE** THAT IS **BLUISH**. ❞

MAKING A FINNISH MARSHMALLOW

Cut a solid piece of dense snow—often called a "marshmallow"—and skewer it with a stick. Secure the stick in the ground close enough to a fire that it receives heat, and position a suitable container underneath it to collect the water as it melts.

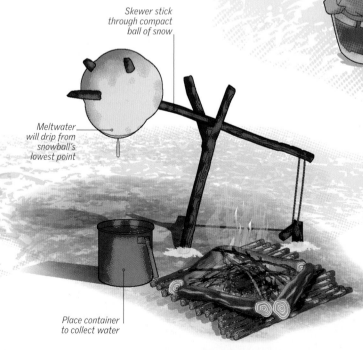

Skewer stick through compact ball of snow

Meltwater will drip from snowball's lowest point

Place container to collect water

USING A MELTING SACK

Based on a principle similar to that of the Finnish marshmallow (see opposite), this technique requires an improvised sack—made from any porous material, such as a T-shirt or sock—suspended near a fire. The heat from the fire will melt the snow, which can then be collected in a container.

Use stick to suspend sack

Make sack from porous material

Suspend sack close enough to fire for it to benefit from heat

USING YOUR FIRE CAN

Even without access to natural fuel for melting ice or snow, if you have your first- or second-line equipment (see p.29), you'll have all you need to procure water. You can set up your fire can (see p.97) on the ground and shelter it from any wind using either your body or your pack. Using your survival can as a container, place small quantities of ice or snow into the can. Light your fire can and place it over the flame. Add more ice or snow as it starts to melt.

> 66 AS LONG AS YOU HAVE YOUR **FIRST- OR SECOND-LINE EQUIPMENT,** YOU CAN PROCURE LIFE-SAVING WATER. 99

Finding water: at sea

Of all environments, the sea is possibly the most difficult in a survival situation. It offers no natural resources for protection against the extremes of temperatures, wind, rain, and sea state, and provides little to aid location. As a result, you should not abandon your vessel unless you absolutely have to.

Collecting fresh water

If you find yourself adrift in your liferaft, with no hope of immediate rescue, obtaining drinking water will be a major priority. Fortunately, even if you don't have a solar still or a reverse-osmosis pump (see pp.142–43), there are several other methods of procuring fresh water.

WARNING

Never drink saltwater. Its salt concentration is three times higher than that of blood and ingesting it will dehydrate you. Continued use over a prolonged period will lead to kidney failure and, ultimately, death.

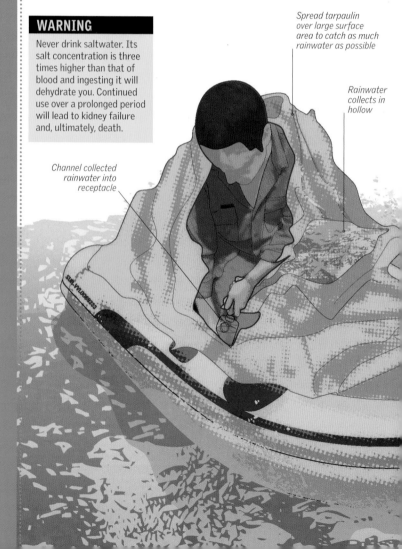

Spread tarpaulin over large surface area to catch as much rainwater as possible

Rainwater collects in hollow

Channel collected rainwater into receptacle

> **"** RETRIEVE AS MUCH **FRESH WATER** AND AS MANY **SIGNALING DEVICES** AS POSSIBLE BEFORE ABANDONING SHIP. **"**

Gathering rainwater

Most modern liferafts have a built-in rainwater catchment system that channels rainwater and dew from the outer surface of the liferaft into pockets inside it. You can also construct a similar system using a tarpaulin or any other waterproof material. Check for any possibility of showers, and spread your tarpaulin in a bowl shape to catch the largest amount of rainwater. Always place a tarpaulin before nightfall, so you don't miss out on any overnight rainfall.

Harvesting dew

At night, secure the tarpaulin like a sunshade and turn up its edges to capture dew. It's also possible to harvest any dew that may have collected on the sides of the raft using a sponge or cloth that you then wring out.

CONSERVING YOUR WATER RATIONS AT SEA

Rationing fresh water supplies is a sensible precaution, since you have no idea how long it will be before you reach land. Here are a few tips to help you conserve what water you have while you're at sea:

• Fix your daily water ration after taking stock of the amount of water you have, the output of solar stills and desalting kits, and the number and physical condition of your party.

• Prevent fresh water supplies from becoming contaminated by saltwater.

• Keep supplies well shaded, both from the sun and the glare off the sea's surface.

• In hot conditions, dampening your clothes with saltwater can help lower your body temperature—but don't overdo this, as continued exposure may lead to saltwater boils and rashes.

• Relax and sleep whenever possible.

• Use every container you have—even a simple garbage bag—to collect rainwater, and keep them sealed and attached to the raft.

• If you don't have water, don't eat. Protein consumption will hasten the onset of dehydration.

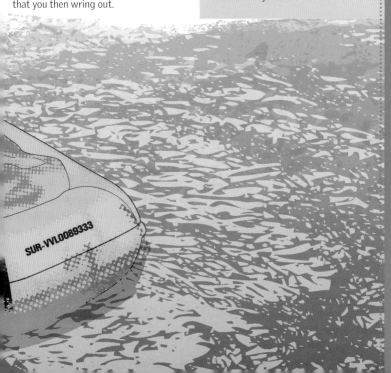

SUR-VVL0089333

Treating saltwater

If you have no means of collecting rainwater or dew, there are several products that can treat saltwater and make it fresh water. Although these products are standard issue on most liferafts, always try to have at least one of them with you when venturing into a marine environment.

Solar still

Solar stills are a simple way of distilling water using the the Sun. Saltwater is placed at the bottom of a container, where it is evaporated by the Sun through clear plastic. Pure water condenses on the top of the plastic and drips down to the side, where it can be collected. Most solar stills on liferafts are inflatable.

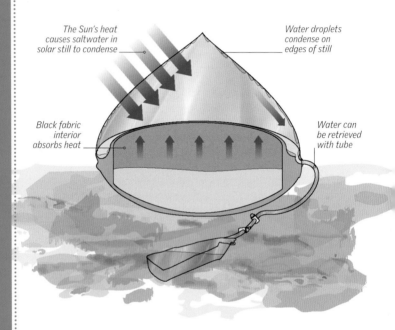

The Sun's heat causes saltwater in solar still to condense

Water droplets condense on edges of still

Black fabric interior absorbs heat

Water can be retrieved with tube

Reverse-osmosis pump

These hand-powered devices pump seawater at a very high pressure through a membrane that filters out the salt. They can produce around 23 quarts (23 liters) of fresh water per day.

Desalting kit

These kits turn seawater into fresh water through "ion exchange." Because they only produce small amounts of fresh water over several hours, use desalting kits only when you can't use a solar still.

❝ REVERSE-OSMOSIS PUMPS ARE HARD WORK; TO AVOID LOSING WATER THROUGH PERSPIRATION, SHARE THE TASK. ❞

Make your own solar still

If you have a chance to gather together the right materials, it's easy to make a solar still. You need two containers (one larger than the other), a plastic sheet, string, and a weight to form a natural run-off point for the water as it condenses under the Sun's heat. If you have some surgical tubing, use it to retrieve the fresh water without taking the still apart.

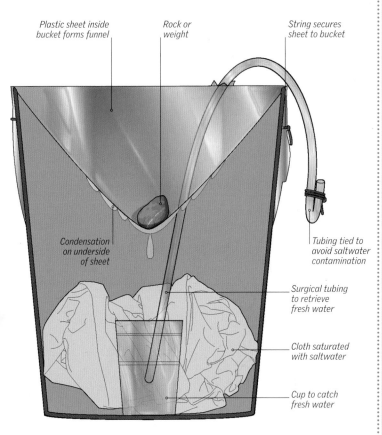

Plastic sheet inside
bucket forms funnel

Rock or
weight

String secures
sheet to bucket

Condensation
on underside
of sheet

Tubing tied to
avoid saltwater
contamination

Surgical tubing
to retrieve
fresh water

Cloth saturated
with saltwater

Cup to catch
fresh water

THE LAST RESORT

In dire situations, you can find potentially life-saving forms of liquid in the ocean.

SEA ICE

In Arctic seas, you can get drinkable water from icebergs (though these are dangerous to approach) and old sea ice, which is bluish, has rounded corners, and splinters easily.

FISH

Cut a fish in half to get to the aqueous fluid found along the spine and in its eye. Don't drink the other fluids: they are rich in protein and fat, and will dehydrate you.

SEA TURTLE

Sea turtle blood has a salt concentration similar to humans. The blood can be collected by slitting the turtle's throat. Note that although this may help prolong survival, sea turtles are an endangered species, so kill one only in an absolute emergency.

REHYDRATION ENEMA

If your water is not salty or poisonous, but too foul to take orally, you can absorb a pint a day—enough to keep you alive—through the large intestine using an improvised tubing device.

Treating water

With the exception of rainwater, all water procured in a survival situation should be treated before drinking, to remove or destroy harmful pathogens and microorganisms.

Filtering water

If you don't have a device that filters and disinfects water, you will have to accomplish the same task in two stages. Before purifying the water, you will have to filter it to remove any debris. You could use a Millbank bag (see box, opposite), but it may be necessary for you to construct your own filter.

Building a tripod filter

To make an improvised filter, you need three sticks for a tripod, and some material to create three separate layers.

1 Use three sticks or a bent sapling to form a tripod. Using any materials you have, form layers, starting at the top with the coarsest material and working your way down using finer materials— such as parachute silk—as you go.

2 Pour water into the top layer. It will become filtered as it passes through the increasingly fine materials.

> EVEN **FILTERED WATER SHOULD BE DISINFECTED** BEFORE DRINKING.

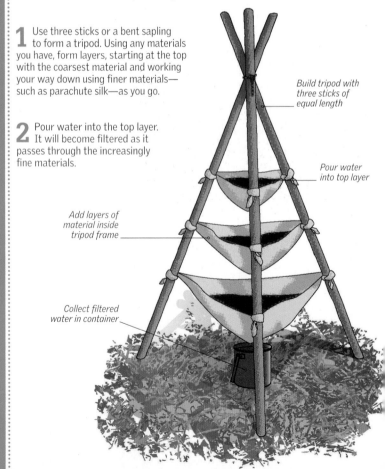

Build tripod with three sticks of equal length

Pour water into top layer

Add layers of material inside tripod frame

Collect filtered water in container

Making a bottle filter

To make an improvised bottle filter, take a container, such as a plastic bottle, and cut off the bottom (or make a hole). Note that a sock used in the same manner is also effective.

1 Hang the bottle upside down from a branch. Fill the bottle with layers of different materials, working from coarse to fine as you work your way down the container.

2 Pour the water into the top end of the bottle and allow it to work its way down through the layers.

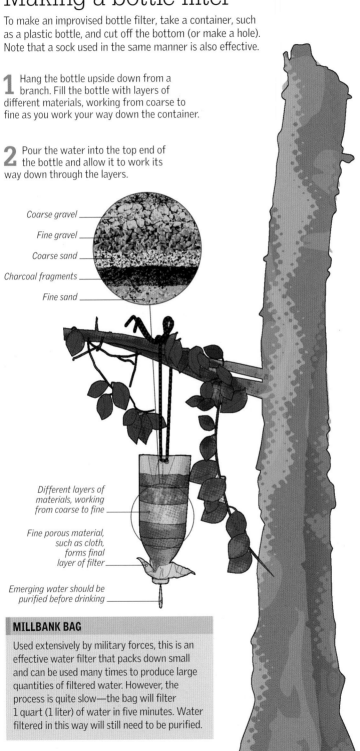

Coarse gravel

Fine gravel

Coarse sand

Charcoal fragments

Fine sand

Different layers of materials, working from coarse to fine

Fine porous material, such as cloth, forms final layer of filter

Emerging water should be purified before drinking

MILLBANK BAG

Used extensively by military forces, this is an effective water filter that packs down small and can be used many times to produce large quantities of filtered water. However, the process is quite slow—the bag will filter 1 quart (1 liter) of water in five minutes. Water filtered in this way will still need to be purified.

Disinfecting water

Drinking untreated water may cause water-borne diseases, so it's vital to treat water first. The most effective way to do this is to boil water. However, if you cannot make a fire, there are several devices available that can filter and purify water. In a survival situation, the availability of water, and your ability to treat, carry, and store it, could be the difference between survival and death.

MINI PORTABLE WATER PURIFIERS

These are specially designed units that filter the water and then purify it, by pumping the contaminated water through either micro-filters, chemicals, or both. Sizes vary from small emergency pumps that purify up to 13 gallons (50 liters) of water, to larger units.

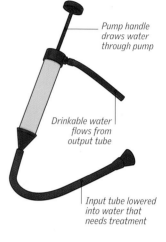

Pump handle draws water through pump

Drinkable water flows from output tube

Input tube lowered into water that needs treatment

Filter system housed inside water bottle

Water passes through filter

GRAVITY/PRESSURE FILTERS

These devices are incorporated within drinking bottles. The water may flow naturally through the system via gravity, or is squeezed through by the operator. These bottles usually employ: a filter to remove sediment and organic contaminants; a micron filter to remove protozoa; and a chemical that kills water-borne bacteria and viruses.

SURVIVAL STRAWS

These compact devices have a filter system and use carbon or iodine resin systems to eliminate diseases and harmful chemicals. You need to get the water to a point where you can reach it with a straw. To draw water to carry, you'll have to draw it into your mouth and decant it into a container.

Place filter end of straw in any accessible non-saline water source

Water sucked through straw

Other methods

If you can't boil water, or if you don't have a water-purification device, you'll have to rely on non-mechanical techniques. The concentration and contact time required for some of these methods is dictated by the quality and temperature of the water being treated.

"BIG BUBBLES, NO TROUBLES"

Microorganisms and virtually all intestinal pathogens are killed at temperatures well below boiling point. The process of bringing water to a boil is sufficient to disinfect it—continuing to boil it just wastes fuel, time, and water.

METHOD	DESCRIPTION
Iodine (Liquid and Tablets)	Iodine effectively destroys bacteria, viruses, and cysts. A concentration of 8mg per quart (liter) at 68°F (20°C) will destroy all pathogens if left for 10 minutes.
Chlorine Tablets	They destroy most bacteria, but are less effective for viruses and cysts. They are more effective when used with phosphoric acid, and will destroy Giardiasis and Cryptosporidium.
Potassium Permanganate	Mix a few granules of this with water until it turns light pink. Leave for at least 30 minutes before drinking.
Bleach	Adding unscented household bleach is the cheapest way to add chlorine to water (it contains 5 percent sodium hypochlorite). Add just one drop of bleach per quart (liter)—two if the water is cloudy. Leave for at least 30 minutes before drinking.
Ultraviolet (UV) Light	In many harmful microorganisms, exposure to UV light disrupts the cell's DNA, rendering the organism harmless. The water's quality impacts the amount of exposure needed.
UV Passive	Fill plastic bottles with water, replace the lids, and place them in direct sunlight on a dark surface to kill the bacteria.
UV Active (Steripen)	This is a small purifier placed in pre-filtered water and activated for a short time. Some models can purify 1 quart (1 liter) in 48 seconds.

" MICROORGANISMS AND INTESTINAL PATHOGENS ARE KILLED AT TEMPERATURES WELL BELOW BOILING POINT. THE PROCESS OF BRINGING WATER TO THE BOIL IS ENOUGH TO DISINFECT IT. "

Extreme survival: at sea

WHAT TO DO

ARE YOU IN DANGER?

• If you are in a group, try to help any others who are in danger

• Prepare to abandon ship, and try to steer closer to either land or known shipping lanes

• Delegate work

• Ensure lifejackets and liferafts are ready

 NO   **YES** ►

Get yourself out of it: **Sinking vessel**—You need water, location aids, and protection from drowning and the elements
Animals—Splashing in water attracts sharks
Injury—Stabilize condition and apply first aid

► **ASSESS YOUR SITUATION** ◄
See pp.154–57

▼

DOES ANYONE KNOW YOU WILL BE MISSING OR WHERE YOU ARE?

If no one knows you are missing or where you are, you must notify people of your plight by any means at your disposal

◄ **NO**   **YES** ►

If you are missed, a rescue party will almost certainly be despatched to find you

▼

DO YOU HAVE ANY MEANS OF COMMUNICATION?

You are faced with surviving for an indefinite period—until you are located or you find help

 NO   **YES** ►

If you have a cell or satellite phone, let someone know your predicament. If your situation is serious enough for emergency rescue, and you have a Personal Locator Beacon (PLB), consider this option

▼

CAN YOU SURVIVE WHERE YOU ARE? *

Abandon ship in a controlled manner and deploy all liferafts. Try to enter the liferaft dry. Use the rescue line to reach people in distress. Follow the "immediate actions" instructions printed inside the liferaft

 NO   **YES** ►

Address the Principles of Survival: Protection; Location; Water; Food

▼   ▼

| YOU WILL HAVE TO MOVE ** | YOU SHOULD STAY ** |

YOU WILL HAVE TO MOVE *

 YOU SHOULD STAY *

▼　　　▼

DO

- Deploy the drogue—this will lessen drifting

- Inventory all food, water, and equipment, and start rationing

- Prepare water procurement devices, such as solar stills and reverse osmosis pumps

- Protect yourself from the Sun, wind, and salt-water spray

- If you have no liferaft, then huddle together in a group with children in the center. If alone, draw your knees up to your chest to lessen heat loss

- Improvise flotation aids from anything that can float or hold trapped air, such as plastic bags or bottles, and knotted or tied clothing

DO

- Ensure that the rescue services are kept aware of your situation and updated with relevant information as the situation dictates

- Prepare to abandon ship: pack lifejackets and suitable clothing

- Ensure you know how to operate your survival equipment and that you have basic aids to location, such as a flashlight, whistle, and plastic water bottle, on your person

- Prepare the vessel for the rescue services, clear the deck of loose objects, and be prepared to drop sail should rescue by helicopter be attempted

- Make an inventory and ration supplies

DON'T

- Cut the painter to the vessel until you know it will sink, as the vessel is what people will be looking for

- Drink seawater under any circumstances—this will only increase your rate of dehydration

- Eat unless you have sufficient water to digest the food—fish is high in protein and requires plenty of water to digest

DON'T

- Neglect to take anti-seasickness tablets. Vomiting will dehydrate you and the effects are very demotivating

- Forget to wear your survival equipment and do make sure everyone knows how to operate it

- Try to second-guess the rescuers when they arrive. Do exactly as they say—they know what they are doing

* If you cannot survive where you are, but you also cannot move because of injury or other factors, you must do everything you can to attract rescue.

** If your situation changes (for instance, you are "moving" to find help, and you find a suitable location in which you can stay and survive) consult the alternative "Dos" and "Don'ts."

In an
Emergency

In an Emergency

You're only a survivor when you have been rescued. This means that you must be able either to get yourself out of the predicament you are in (self-rescue) or be rescued from that situation by others. Sometimes you will be able to choose whether to undertake self-rescue; at other times, the decision will be out of your hands. There may be several reasons why you cannot achieve self-rescue: you could be utterly lost; local conditions such as flooding or bad weather could trap you; or injury to yourself or a group member could make movement impossible. In such a situation, the onus is on you to attract attention.

You must be able to make contact with rescuers, using location aids you have with you or those you can improvise. Never delay any form of rescue because of the embarrassment factor—the only important factor is the outcome, and I would always rather be embarrassed and alive than eventually found dead!

Preparation is key—informing people of your intentions and timeframes will at least have someone wondering why you are not back yet. Equally, taking the best location aids for your environment, and knowing how best to use them, will increase your chances of being found.

In many survival situations, a major decision will be whether to remain where you are or move to a location that offers a better chance of survival, rescue, or both. There are many factors that will dictate your best option but, in general, it's always advisable to stay where you are. It's all too easy to make a rash decision and attempt to walk out of a situation, only to put yourself in even greater danger.

❝ YOU ARE NOT A SURVIVOR UNTIL YOU HAVE RESCUED YOURSELF OR BEEN RESCUED BY OTHERS. ❞

Using a location aid

A location aid can make the difference between life and death. A comparatively recent invention is the multitasking Skystreme device.

Skystreme is an inflatable silver foil kite, which weighs just $1^1/_2$oz (43g) and packs down to a small and convenient size. It can perform four tasks in a survival situation:

1 Location aid: the kite is orally inflated and its wedge shape means it can lift off from the ground unaided in 4mph (6kph) winds.
• The 165ft (50m) of line attached to the kite (this much cordage is invaluable in itself) allows it to rise above tree levels and reflect sunlight. It can be seen by the naked eye at a distance of 2 miles (3km).
• At night, you can hang a small flashlight or Cyalume underneath the kite to aid visibility.
• The metallic surface reflects radar and can be detected by aircraft at a distance of 10 miles (17km). A British Royal Marine on a polar crossing once flew his Skystreme behind his sled so his support aircraft could find and track him!

2 Emergency first aid splint: the kite can be inflated around a broken or sprained limb.

3 Thermal vest: the kite can be inflated and put inside clothing to act as a body warmer.

4 Water storage: instead of being inflated with air, the kite can be used to carry and store water.

Assessing your situation

Once you're out of immediate danger, assess your situation and plan accordingly. At this initial stage, it's crucial to think clearly—the decisions you make now could mean the difference between life and death. In most cases, remaining where you are is the preferred option, but no two situations are ever the same: the circumstances, environment, conditions, and you—the individual—all have a major impact on what can and cannot be achieved.

The strategy for staying alive

In an emergency situation, think of the four priorities of survival: protection, location, water, and food. Your situation will determine which is the most important. In most cases, as long as you're in no further danger from injury or the elements, you should focus your efforts on establishing a safe location and getting yourself rescued. The strategy for staying alive, known by the acronym SURVIVAL (see pp.156–57), gives you a framework to use and helps you remember what you need to do to remain alive and get rescued.

THE RULE OF THREES

The rule of threes can help you focus your decision-making, particularly if you are injured, at risk of further injury, or in immediate danger from the elements. In most cases:
- Three seconds is the psychological reaction time for making a decision.
- Three minutes is the length of time your brain can do without oxygen before it suffers irreparable damage.
- Three hours is the critical time you can survive unprotected in extreme climates.
- Three days is the approximate length of time you can live without water.
- Three weeks is the approximate length of time you can live without food.

"IT CAN BE ALL TOO EASY TO MAKE A RASH DECISION AND TRY TO WALK OUT OF A SITUATION ONLY TO PUT YOURSELF IN EVEN GREATER DANGER."

THE ENEMIES OF SURVIVAL

In a survival situation, these seven factors, known as "the enemies of survival" can work against you if you aren't mentally prepared. You can memorize these by using a mnemonic such as: "Be Prepared To Face These Hostile Factors."

Boredom and Loneliness	When boredom sets in, you become inactive and lose the ability to deal with your situation effectively, so you need to keep busy. Loneliness can add to the magnitude of your tasks, leading to a feeling of helplessness.
Pain	If you're injured, don't ignore the pain. Attend to a minor injury, as it could grow into a major problem. A positive attitude coupled with keeping busy helps to distract the mind from pain.
Thirst	Thirst is not a good indicator of the body's need for water. Stay ahead of dehydration and prioritize your need for water according to your environment.
Fatigue	Tiredness leads to mistakes that, at best, cause frustration, and at worst, may result in injury or death. Never underestimate the importance of quality rest to your physical and mental well-being.
Temperature	You should dress to suit the environment you're in and be aware of the signs and symptoms of temperature-related conditions, such as hypothermia and heat stroke.
Hunger	In a short-term survival situation (one to five days), procuring food is not a high priority as long as you drink water and pace yourself to work within your limits. However, take every opportunity to procure food without expending energy.
Fear	Fear is one of our body's greatest survival tools since it can stimulate you, so that you're ready to act—however, it can also debilitate. Fear is good as long as you have control over it, and the key to controlling fear in a survival situation is knowledge.

"SURVIVAL"—the strategy for staying alive

SIZE UP YOUR SITUATION	**S**	• Assess the particulars of your surroundings, physical condition, and equipment. If you're in a group, you can share tasks and responsibilities.
USE ALL YOUR SENSES	**U**	• Most people react to a true survival situation through either training or by instinct. • Listen to your subconscious survival senses and gut feelings.
REMEMBER WHERE YOU ARE	**R**	• In any survival situation, it always helps to know where you are so that you can make the best decisions about what to do and where to go next.
VANQUISH FEAR	**V**	• Fear and panic can be formidable enemies, so it's imperative that you have the knowledge and training to counteract them and prevent them from making your situation worse.
IMPROVISE	**I**	• The true skill of a survivor is to understand what's required and improvise solutions to particular problems. Do you have the skills to be proactive in your own rescue?
VALUE LIVING AND LIFE	**V**	• Some people without training and equipment have survived the most horrendous situations. In many cases, this was simply because they had the will to live.
ACT LIKE THE LOCALS	**A**	• Whatever environment you're trying to survive in, you can be sure that the indigenous people and the local wildlife have developed ways of adapting to it in order to survive.
LEARN BASIC SKILLS	**L**	• Learning basic skills increases your chances of survival. Without training, your prospects of survival are down to luck, which is never the best place to start.

- Every environment has its own particular characteristics—hot/dry/cold/wet. Determine what you need to do to adapt to that environment.
- Assess how your equipment can be used best.
- Remove yourself and others from danger.

- Whatever has happened, approach your predicament in a calm and rational manner. The situation requires careful thought and planning.
- If you act in haste, you may overlook important factors, lose vital equipment, or simply make matters worse. The saying "Undue haste makes waste" is especially true in a survival situation.

- Knowing your precise location can clarify whether rescuers are likely to find you (see pp.18–19) or if you'll have to rescue yourself. It can also give you an idea of the obstacles you may face.
- Channel your efforts into making sure that when rescuers are looking for you, your aids to location are in place.

- If uncontrolled, fear and panic can destroy your ability to make rational decisions, they can cause you to react to your feelings and imagination rather than to your actual situation.
- If you're in a group, your responses can directly affect others—positive responses are productive and can motivate.

- You may start out with all the right equipment, but it may get lost or broken, or simply wear out. Your ability to improvise may help you in your struggle to survive in relative comfort.
- Think laterally—like the climber stranded on the side of a mountain, who used the flash on his camera to signal to a rescue helicopter.

- The stories of prisoners of war often reveal what kept them alive: religious beliefs, thoughts of family and friends, or a determination not to let the enemy win.
- If the will to live is not there, then just having the knowledge and equipment may not be enough.

- Look at how the local people dress and act: in hot countries, they leave manual work until the coolest parts of the day and work slowly to reduce sweating and therefore, conserve water.
- In a jungle, pay attention when the animals become quiet or quickly leave an area—danger is usually around the corner.

- Prior preparation is the key to survival: discover what you need to know about the environment you're going to; familiarize yourself with your equipment; and practice your basic skills until they become second nature. This thorough preparation will help you to combat the fear of the unknown and increase your self-confidence.

Attracting rescuers

To be a survivor, you need to rescue yourself or be rescued by others. If you can't rescue yourself—perhaps you're injured, completely lost, or trapped by bad weather—you must attract attention with location aids that you've either brought with you or have improvised.

Aids to location

Location aids can save your life, so make sure you know how to use them effectively. A helicopter on a search pattern may make only one pass over an area before moving on, so you'll only have a few minutes to act decisively.

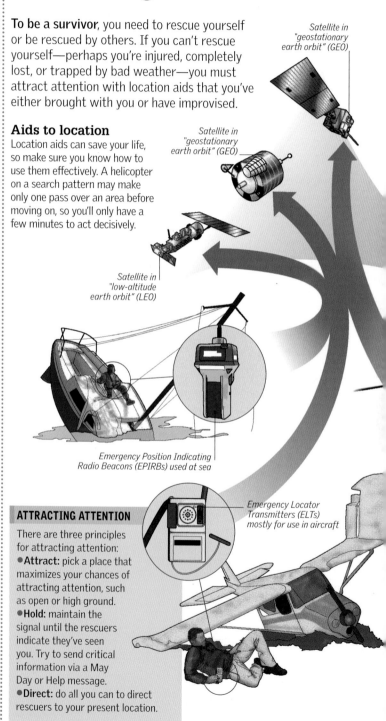

Satellite in "geostationary earth orbit" (GEO)

Satellite in "geostationary earth orbit" (GEO)

Satellite in "low-altitude earth orbit" (LEO)

Emergency Position Indicating Radio Beacons (EPIRBs) used at sea

Emergency Locator Transmitters (ELTs) mostly for use in aircraft

ATTRACTING ATTENTION

There are three principles for attracting attention:
- **Attract:** pick a place that maximizes your chances of attracting attention, such as open or high ground.
- **Hold:** maintain the signal until the rescuers indicate they've seen you. Try to send critical information via a May Day or Help message.
- **Direct:** do all you can to direct rescuers to your present location.

Communicating with satellites

When activated, a Personal Locator Beacon (PLB) transmits a radio distress signal to two complementary satellite systems called LEOSAR and GEOSAR. Together, these form the "COSPAS-SARSAT" system. The signal is then relayed to a rescue coordination center closest to the beacon's location.

CELL TELEPHONES AND RADIOS
Always take a cell or satellite phone with you when traveling. On a sea trip, take a marine VHF radio.

CELL AND SATELLITE PHONES
Choose a cell phone with a GPS unit to fix and track your position, and a camera to send pictures of your location and any injuries. Or, buy a satellite phone connected to the Iridium Satellite Phone System.

MARINE VHF RADIOS
These handheld units transmit and receive on frequencies between 156 to 174 MHz, usually on Channel 16, the international calling and distress channel. Your device should be waterproof, able to float, and kept on charge.

Local User Terminals (LUTs) receive signals from satellites and alert mission control

Mission control analyzes data from LUTs and mobilizes rescue operation

Regional rescue coordination center alerts search-and-rescue teams

Search-and-rescue services deployed to search for you

PLB, activated manually, sends signal to search-and-rescue satellite

Personal Locator Beacons (PLBs), for personal use, are kept on body

WARNING
PLBs are for emergency use only and should always be used responsibly.

Making a dome signal fire

A **well-made**, well-located signal fire generates enough smoke to be seen from afar. To make a dome signal fire, build a large fire on a raised platform under a dome-shaped structure made from bent saplings. If you don't have saplings, use poles to make a teepee shape.

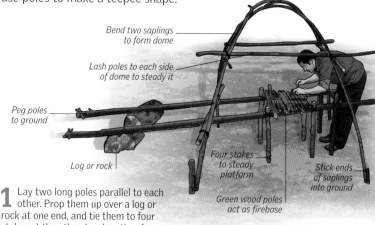

Bend two saplings to form dome

Lash poles to each side of dome to steady it

Peg poles to ground

Log or rock

Four stakes to steady platform

Green wood poles act as firebase

Stick ends of saplings into ground

1 Lay two long poles parallel to each other. Prop them up over a log or rock at one end, and tie them to four stakes at the other. Lay lengths of green wood side by side on the poles.
- Bend two long saplings at 90 degrees to each other to form a dome.

Tinder, kindling, fuel, and vegetation

2 Prepare a fire (see pp.98–99) on the platform and load it with green vegetation.
- Lay the vegetation close enough to the fuel below to catch easily when the fire is lit—but don't smother it.

Stab branch or vine into bundle, wrap it around and tuck it under itself

3 Prepare kindling to turn the initial flame into a fire. Make kindling by breaking small, dead branches from the lower trunks of trees. Fold them into a bundle held together by a thin branch or vine.

SIGNAL FIRE ESSENTIALS

Follow these principles to make your signal fire as effective as possible.

FIRE FORMATION

Build three fires in a recognized formation of a triangle or a straight line. They should be at least 65ft (20m) apart.

FIRE COMPONENTS

• Site the firebase off the ground to keep out dampness, and to allow enough airflow for it to ignite effectively.

• Cover the top of the firebase with green vegetation and anything else that makes smoke. This keeps the firebase dry.

AT THE READY

Keep the following nearby:
• Dry tinder in a waterproof container.
• Hexamine fuel tablets, stove fuel, gasoline, paper, or birch bark.
• A witch's broom, made of a cleft stick stuffed with kindling or bark, so you can quickly light the broom and transfer it to the signal fire.

4 Layer green vegetation on top of the dome to form a roof over the fire platform.
• Keep additional green vegetation nearby to add to the fire.

Leave access point for lighting fire, but keep it closed so tinder, kindling, and fuel stay dry

Make witch's broom out of kindling or bark

Orange smoke from flare mingles with fire smoke, increasing its visibility

5 Light a witch's broom (see panel, top) from your camp fire, take it to the dome, and light the fire.
• Use your kindling (see Step 3) to help get the fire going.

6 When smoke billows upward, light a preprepared signal flare (see p.163), if you have one, taped or tied to a long pole.
• Use the pole to position the flare as high into the smoke as you can.

Other rescue signals

In addition to signal fires, there are other visual devices for attracting potential rescuers. Some are unusual and others, such as a whistle, quite obvious. Whatever device you use, you have to try to hold the rescuers' attention by persisting with your signal.

Light windmill

You can create a highly visible, illuminated "windmill" effect (see below) by whirling in front of you a chemical lightstick (cyalume) attached to the end of a cord 3ft (1m) long. Depending on local conditions, it can be seen up to 2 miles (3km) away—or farther by an aircraft crew. Blow your whistle at the same time, using the International Distress Signal of six blasts over one minute, then one minute's silence. The reply is three short blasts.

Tinsel tree

This is effective only during daylight hours, and is best used when you're in one place for a while. Cut a silver survival blanket or any reflective material into strips. Attach them to a tree so they move in the breeze and catch the sunlight, glinting like mirrors.

Lightstick filled with luminous substance known as cyalume

Activate lightstick and whirl it in front of you

GROUND-TO-AIR MARKERS

You can improvise internationally recognized emergency signals on the ground that rescuers in the air can see.

GETTING NOTICED

Use anything that contrasts with the ground, such as orange lifejackets.
• Make sure the message is big and visible from all directions.
• Use one of the emergency codes shown on the right. SOS or HELP written in big letters will attract attention, too.

V	Require assistance
X	Require medical assistance
N	No/Negative
Y	Yes/Affirmative
↑	Proceed this way (arrow points)

Signaling distress

Two of the most recognized signs of distress are a little red star shooting up into the sky or a billowing cloud of orange smoke. There are many types of signal flare and rocket, ranging from simple, handheld devices that fire flares into the sky to specialized kits designed to penetrate jungle canopy.

SIGNAL FLARES

One end of a signal flare has an orange-colored smoke signal for daytime use. The other end has a flare for nighttime use, but it can be used during the day as well. Follow the instructions on the outside of the device and wear gloves to protect your hands. The heat from a flare can damage a liferaft, so keep your flare clear when you light it. Make sure you don't discard flares unless you have used both ends.

Whistle

Take a whistle when you go out into the wilderness because sound, especially in areas where there's little noise pollution, travels great distances. Tie the whistle around your neck (see pp.28–29).

To use whistle for international distress call, see Light Windmill (opposite)

Hold signal flare as high as you can to make it more visible

Extreme survival: in cold conditions

WHAT TO DO

ARE YOU IN DANGER?

If you are in a group, try to help any others who are in danger

◀ NO   YES ▶

Get yourself out of it:
Cold/wind/wet—Get yourself out of these elements as they can lead to hypothermia
Animals—Avoid confrontation; move away from danger
Injury—Stabilize condition and apply first aid

ASSESS YOUR SITUATION ◀
See pp.154–57

DOES ANYONE KNOW YOU WILL BE MISSING OR WHERE YOU ARE?

If no one knows you are missing or where you are, you must notify people of your plight by any means at your disposal

◀ NO   YES ▶

If you are missed, a rescue party will almost certainly be despatched to find you

DO YOU HAVE ANY MEANS OF COMMUNICATION?

You are faced with surviving for an indefinite period—until you are located or you find help

◀ NO   YES ▶

If you have a cell or satellite phone, let someone know your predicament. If your situation is serious enough for emergency rescue, and you have a Personal Locator Beacon (PLB), consider this option

CAN YOU SURVIVE WHERE YOU ARE? *

If you cannot survive where you are and there are no physical reasons why you should remain, you'll have to move to a location that offers a better chance of survival, rescue, or both

◀ NO   YES ▶

Address the Principles of Survival: Protection; Location; Water; Food

YOU WILL HAVE TO MOVE **

YOU SHOULD STAY **

YOU WILL HAVE TO MOVE * **YOU SHOULD STAY ***

▼ ▼

DO

- Make an informed decision on the best location to move to
- Keep hydrated by wrapping snow in a wet item of clothing and suck it as it melts—but only if you are walking or working and generating heat
- Improvise a walking stick that can be used to check the depth and quality of snow, and unseen drop-offs
- Check regularly for signs of frost nip or frostbite, and hypothermia
- Have aids to location accessible while moving and distributed while static
- Protect all your extremities from the elements—tie gloves to cord threaded through your jacket so they don't get lost

DO

- Select a suitable shelter site away from dangers. Build it big enough for you and your equipment. Incorporate a cold sink and a sleeping platform higher than the sink
- Keep cutting and digging tools in the shelter in case very heavy snowfall or an avalanche requires you to dig your way out
- Mark the entrance to the shelter so you can find it easily
- Keep a fire going: once established, you can use it to melt snow and benefit from the warmth
- Prepare all of your aids to location for immediate use

DON'T

- Underestimate the need for water just because it is cold—you are just as likely to get dehydrated in a cold environment as in a hot one
- Post-hole through virgin snow—it is exhausting. Instead, improvise a pair of snow shoes
- Sleep directly on the ground. Ventilate your shelter and check for natural dangers (such as an avalanche)

DON'T

- Use your body heat to melt snow since it lowers your body temperature and can induce hypothermia
- Breathe air onto cold hands—breath contains moisture which will then cool and conduct heat away from your hands
- Sit or lie directly on the cold ground. Use whatever is available to improvise a sitting or sleeping platform

* If you cannot survive where you are, but you also cannot move because of injury or other factors, you must do everything you can to attract rescue.

** If your situation changes (for instance, you are "moving" to find help, and you find a suitable location in which you can stay and survive) consult the alternative "Dos" and "Don'ts."

First aid essentials

Before you set off, check that you have the necessary medical equipment—especially medications. Personal hygiene is vital for protection—it ensures your body is efficient and reduces health risks. How you feel physically also directly impacts how you feel psychologically. It is worthwhile to go on a first aid training course, and take a comprehensive manual with you.

WARNING

Protect yourself from danger at all times. You can't help anyone if you become a casualty as well. If the area is unsafe, get help and monitor the casualty's condition from a safe distance.

Basic first aid kit

Keep your first aid kit (see panel, opposite) dry and readily accessible. Check that the seals on sterile dressings are intact. Quickly replace anything you use.

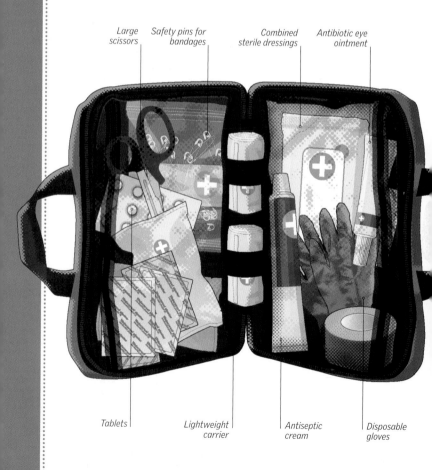

Large scissors

Safety pins for bandages

Combined sterile dressings

Antibiotic eye ointment

Tablets

Lightweight carrier

Antiseptic cream

Disposable gloves

Zinc-oxide tape to secure dressings

Take fabric, waterproof, and hypoallergenic bandages

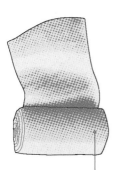

Reusable gauze roller bandage

CHECKLIST
Make sure that your first aid kit and medicines are suited to the environment you will be visiting.

BASIC KIT
- Alcohol-free antiseptic wipes
- Latex-free disposable gloves
- Alcohol gel for handwashing
- Antiseptic cream
- Antibiotic eye ointment
- Adhesive dressings—fabric, waterproof, and hypoallergenic
- Gel blister bandages
- Combined sterile dressings, or sterile pads and bandages in assorted sizes
- Roller bandages—take self-adhesive for supporting joints and gauze for securing dressings
- Two triangular bandages
- Micropore or zinc-oxide tape
- Scissors and tweezers
- Safety pins
- Disposable syringes

PERSONAL MEDICATION
- Painkillers and anti-inflammatories
- Medical alert bracelet/pendant
- Prescription medicines such as asthma inhaler and/or adrenaline (epinephrine) auto-injector
- Antihistamines
- Anti-diarrhea medicine
- Packets of oral rehydration salts
- Hydrocortisone cream

ENVIRONMENT-SPECIFIC EXTRAS
- Malaria tablets
- Mosquito repellent
- Anti-poison-ivy cream
- Sunblock
- Tick remover
- DEET powder for removing leeches

PRIORITIES AFTER AN INCIDENT
Assess a situation quickly and methodically. Check casualties for life-threatening conditions such as unconsciousness or severe bleeding and treat those first. If the casualty is responding to you, he or she is conscious. If you're not sure, shake the shoulders gently. Check the airway—if the casualty can talk, it is open and clear; otherwise, open and clear it. See if breathing is normal and treat difficulties such as asthma. If the casualty is unconscious and not breathing, call for help and begin CPR. Once life-threatening conditions are under control, make a more detailed assessment. Finding out how the incident occurred can indicate likely injuries.

Protecting against infection

Disposable gloves prevent cross-infection between you and the casualty; they must be latex-free, since contact with latex can cause an allergic reaction. Antiseptic wipes are also invaluable when cleaning wounds.

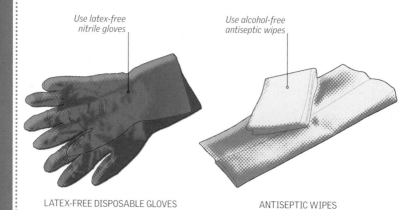

Use latex-free nitrile gloves

Use alcohol-free antiseptic wipes

LATEX-FREE DISPOSABLE GLOVES

ANTISEPTIC WIPES

COMBINED STERILE DRESSING

This is a sealed dressing consisting of a pad attached to a bandage. It's easy to apply, and can be used as a sling. It should be taped to your backpack strap for easy access in an emergency.

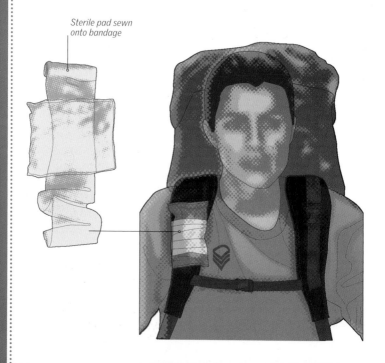

Sterile pad sewn onto bandage

Improvised slings

Hand, arm, or shoulder injuries need to be immobilized and supported in a raised position. If you don't have a triangular bandage, use strong cloth about 3ft (1m) square, folded in half to form a triangle. You can also use your jacket or backpack straps. Ask the casualty to support the arm with their other hand while you secure the sling.

JACKET CORNER
To support an injured forearm or hand, fold the jacket up over the arm and pin it.

BUTTON-UP JACKET
Undo one of the buttons and slide the injured arm into the opening for support.

SHOULDER STRAP
Rest a sprain by tucking your hand in your backpack strap.

PINNED SLEEVE
Pin your sleeve to the jacket or the strap of a backpack for support.

BELT SUPPORT
Support an upper arm injury in a raised position with a belt looped into a figure eight.

❝ MOST INJURIES CAN EITHER BE DEALT WITH OR STABILIZED USING **BASIC FIRST AID** AND **COMMON SENSE**. ❞

Index

Acknowledgments

About the author

After joining the Royal Navy in 1977, Colin Towell qualified as a Combat Survival Instructor with 22 Regiment SAS, and has spent over 30 years teaching land, sea, desert, jungle, and cold-weather survival skills—as well as survival and conduct in captivity—to UK Army, Navy, Royal Marines, and Air Force personnel. He was the Royal Navy's Chief Survival Instructor and also served three years as Chief Instructor at the US Navy SERE (Survival, Evasion, Resistance, and Extraction) school. Colin saw service in the Falklands, Bosnia, Germany, USA, and Northern Ireland, and still serves as a Reserve Chief Instructor with the UK Defence SERE Training Organisation, training both instructors and students. He provided the survival training, equipment, and rescue coordination for Sir Richard Branson's balloon global circumnavigation attempts, and also trials, evaluates, and instructs in the use of specialized survival equipment, both in the UK and abroad.

www.colintowell-survival.com

From the author

My warm thanks go to the following people for generously sharing their expertise:
Flt. Lt. John Hudson, Royal Air Force, Defence SERE Training Centre; Lt. Carlton Oliver, Royal Navy, Defence SERE Training Centre; Tony Borkowski (Royal School Military Survey); Mike Dymond M.R.I.N N.DipM (RYA); Robert (Baldy Bob) Whale; Charlie Tyrrell; Colin Knox (Pre-Mac); Murray Bryars; Paul Baker (Bushman.UK Knifes); and Mr. Kimball White. Finally, I would like to thank the Defence SERE Organisation and the Survival Equipment Branch of the Royal Navy for giving me an amazing career.

From the publisher

Dorling Kindersley would like to thank Lt. Cdr. Stuart Antrobus at the Royal Navy and Olivia Smales at IMG. Thanks also to Mike Garland, Darren Awuah, Phil Gamble, Peter Liddiard, Tim Loughead, and Mark Walker for the illustrations, Adam Brackenbury for creative technical support, and Margaret McCormack for indexing.

“ TREAT THE **WILDERNESS** WITH **RESPECT**: CARRY IN ONLY WHAT YOU ARE PREPARED TO **CARRY OUT**; LEAVE ONLY **FOOTPRINTS**; TAKE ONLY **PICTURES**. **”**